1

"Eat food. Not too much. Mostly Plants." - Michael Pollan

EATING WHOLE

Easy & Healthy Whole Food Plant Based Recipes

by Michele Swaczyna founder of Vegan Michele

Welcome and thank you so much for purchasing **Eating Whole**. I am so excited to share the wonderful world of healthy whole plant foods and the power they contain to not only help you lose weight, but come to a place of overall health and longevity. In my other cookbook **Be Vegan - Skip the Diet, Just Eat Healthy** I included some great tasting, basic and easy to prepare vegan meals for all to enjoy. But since then I have been dreaming of creating a cookbook that takes into account the tenants of weight loss and how to go about losing weight as I know so many people out there struggle with excess weight they would like to shed. My passion is helping people on their weight loss journey and I desired to have a cookbook reflecting the practices I teach in my Holistic Nutrition Business. I wanted it to be easy for people to follow as a meal plan, or to just have some more healthy, yet still super delicious oil free, whole food plant based recipes in their arsenal to be able to succeed.

We all want to live our days with health, vitality, and energy to reach whatever goals we are trying to achieve in life. After working with hundreds of weight loss clients, there is one thing I have seen to be consistently true: conquer your weight loss goals, and you find the confidence in your ability to tackle pretty much any other goals you have. So think of this book as a starting point.

I've put my heart and soul into creating these delicious and creative recipes as well as curating concise information to get you started on your health and weight loss journey. So let's begin.

With Love,

Michele .

DISCLAIMER: The Eating Whole 28 day meal plan is not a customized weight loss plan that will work perfectly for everyone. It is merely a template that can help you get started while you figure out the best way to eat a WFPBD that suits YOUR specific needs and tastes. I created the Eating Whole 28 day meal plan specifically to help those struggling to shed unhealthy weight. But the recipes can be used in a way that suits your life, and you can feel free to mix up the days and meals as you see fit. I am a Certified Holistic Nutritionist and have created this book to be a balanced approach to weight loss, but as always, please consult your health care provider upon embarking on any new dietary changes.

CONTENTS

For products and kitchen tools I used in this book, please check out my Amazon Store Front. You can also find my favorite Vegan Beauty and Self Care items, and books to keep you motivated on your journey to health:

(a) amazon.com/shop/veganmichele

For additional resources and free recipes:

𝕏 veganmichele.com
▶ youtube.com/veganmichele
◉ instagram.com/vegan_michele
ⓕ facebook.com/veganmichele

INTRODUCTION

The book is divided into four sections: I start out with some foundational information about eating a whole food plant based diet, then give tips to set you up on your weight loss journey. Next, the 28 Day Meal Plan and all the recipes that will support weight loss yet keep you satisfied. The recipes are organized into seven sections: *Breakfast, Soups and Beans, Salads and Dressings, Dips, Spreads and Toppings, Wraps Sandwiches and Bowls, Main Dishes, Desserts and Warm Drinks*. I have a few healthy dessert recipes you can throw in on occasion that will not derail your weigh loss efforts, BUT these are not for every single day if you are serious about shedding excess weight. Feel free to mix things up and eat according to your own body's needs and hunger levels.

The 28 Day Meal Plan is a nutrient dense meal plan I've designed as a guide if you'd like to have a plan to follow. It will help you "reset" your body and reach your weight loss goals. It's up to you to decide if you want to jump in and commit to the challenge for the full 28 days, or you can simply try one recipe at a time and move at your own pace.

Remember to use this as a guide or a "starting point" and tailor it to your specific needs based on what works best for your life. If you find a few meals that you LOVE that are easy for you to prepare and you want to eat them every day for a week, go for it! Weeks 1 and 2 provide a mix of brand new recipes. Weeks 3 and 4 will be a mixture of my personal favorites.

SECTION 1 - WHOLE FOOD PLANT BASED FOUNDATIONS

What exactly does it mean to eat Whole Food Plant Based? Why is it different than Vegan?

A **whole food plant based diet** is centered on whole, unrefined or minimally refined plant foods and excludes or minimizes meat, dairy products, eggs, and highly refined foods such as bleached white flour, refined sugar, and oil. A person eating this way will eat mainly fruits, vegetables (including tubers and starchy vegetables), whole grains, and legumes.

A **vegan diet** totally eliminates all animal products. Over time, more and more people have started to adopt the vegan way of eating for reasons other than animal welfare, and today a "vegan diet" is commonly used to describe a diet that excludes animal products, regardless of motivation.

The "whole food" part of "whole food, plant based" has become increasingly relevant, as highly processed vegan foods have become more widely available, making it possible to eat a vegan diet while eating very few whole plant foods. It's not just possible but common to be both vegan and whole food plant based, which is what I personally do. Many people adopt a whole food plant based diet and, after experiencing dramatic health benefits, become interested in other reasons for avoiding animal products, such as the environmental impact and ethical issues surrounding factory farming. I have also spoken to many vegans who gave up animal products for ethical reasons and, after some time, decided to adopt a whole food plant based diet for their health.

Why Whole Plant Foods?

The optimal human diet for health and longevity is 100% whole foods with 90% coming from plant based sources. Eating lots of fruits, veggies, whole grains, beans and legumes, and some nuts and seeds. Cutting out highly processed foods (ex. processed sugars, refined white flours, and oils).

I choose to be 100% vegan, but if you choose to eat animal products, keep them to less than 10% of your calories. Think of the whole plant foods as the main meal and the animal products as the condiments. For example, you may choose to have a piece of chicken or fish once a week This would be an acceptable way you could still reap all of the health benefits of eating this way 90% of the time while adding in a few animal sources.

What is a Whole Food or an Unprocessed Food?

Think of these as "real" foods. They are essentially intact, close to the form in which they grew. None of their nutritious parts have been removed, and nothing unhealthy has been added to them. They include whole fruits and vegetables, whole grains, beans, legumes, nuts, and seeds. They normally do not come packaged, and you will find them in the perimeter of most grocery stores. It is important to note when it comes to weight loss, although considered "whole" foods I would caution against consuming too many of the calorie dense whole foods like avocados, nuts, seeds, olives, and dried fruits.

What do Highly Processed and Minimally Processed mean?

Highly Processed Foods - These foods have been significantly altered from their original state. Stripped of fiber, and other essential parts, they are often packed with added salt, fat, sugar, chemicals and are calorie rich but nutrient poor. Examples include refined grains like white flour, white pasta, cookies, packaged chips and snack foods, candy, sweets, anything deep fried etc. For weight loss you want to completely eliminate these foods.

Minimally Processed Foods - Some processing has still occurred, but the food is still fairly intact and has not been overly stripped of its nutritional value. Many of these still contain all of the parts of the whole food, but have been broken down into smaller pieces. I do use minimally processed ingredients in this cookbook that are deemed to still be a very healthy choice and can give you variety in your meals. Some examples would be a brown rice pasta, corn tortillas, tofu and tempeh, or nut butters. As with anything packaged, be sure to read the ingredient list and try to choose the option with the least ingredients possible. Too much added sugar, oil or salt can turn a simple plant food into a junk food fast.

Why No Oil?

This often comes as a surprise to most people beginning their whole food plant based journey, and many have been led to believe that oils are actually health foods. The reason for this is because oils (ex. canola oil, olive oil, sunflower oil, corn oil, coconut oil, vegan margarines etc.) are nutrient poor devoid of any nutritional value beyond fat. They have been extracted in such a way that removes the beneficial nutrients of the whole food they were extracted from (nutrients along with fiber, leaving only empty calories). In addition, oils are among one of the most calorie dense foods on the planet and truly destroy any traction you might have when trying to lose weight. Learning to limit or set the oil aside completely will help getting and staying in shape much easier.

Once you get the hang of cooking without oil, I promise you will not miss it in the slightest. All of the recipes in this book are oil free and still extremely tasty.

Foods to Incorporate Daily

Whole Grains (ex. barley, brown rice, quinoa, popcorn, oats, whole grain pastas, wild rice, millet, rye, spelt etc.)

Beans and Other Legumes (ex. black, pinto, cannellini, chickpeas, green peas, edamame, great northern, kidney, lentils, split peas, tempeh)

Berries (ex. acai, blueberries, blackberries, strawberries, cherries, cranberries, goji, raspberries etc.)

Other Fruits (ex. apples, apricots, mangoes, bananas, peaches, oranges, papaya, watermelon etc.)

Cruciferous Vegetables (ex. kale, brussels sprouts, cabbage, cauliflower, broccoli, watercress, bok choy etc.)

Leafy Greens (ex. spinach, lettuces, collard greens, swiss chard, mustard greens, kale, sorrel etc.)

Other Vegetables (ex. corn, carrots, zucchini, squash, tomatoes, potatoes, sweet potatoes, sea vegetables, mushrooms, peppers etc.)

A Small Amount of Nuts and Seeds (ex. flaxseeds, chia seeds, hemp seeds, pumpkin seeds, walnuts, cashews, almonds etc.)

Spices and Herbs (ex. turmeric, basil, cinnamon, parsley, pepper, cumin, curry powder, dill, paprika, vanilla, thyme, rosemary etc.)

But, Where Do You Get Your Protein?

Plants. Contain. Protein. Beans, legumes, whole grains, leafy greens, vegetables, seeds, nuts all contain wonderful sources of protein. In fact, a greater consumption of animal protein has been linked to increased mortality and a host of other diseases (See the book "The China Study"), while a greater consumption of plant protein has been associated with a longer life span. Most people are concerned with not getting enough protein, however are unaware of how much they already get, and what is the amount needed for optimal health. Government recommendations are 46 grams of protein for the average woman, and 56 grams of protein for the average man, but the majority of people are actually getting much more on a daily basis causing stress to the systems in our bodies and making the liver and kidneys overwork. It is virtually impossible to be protein deficient if you are eating enough calories. So just make sure you are eating enough whole plant foods to feel satisfied. Eating lots of whole plant foods not only provides you with enough, it safe guards you from getting too much.

What Supplements to Include?

Often times people are scared that switching to a plant based diet will leave them lacking nutrients, but keeping your diet varied eating a plethora of different plant foods will allow you to get a full spectrum of nutrition. The one nutrient that is indisputably lacking in a vegan or mostly plant based diet is **B-12** and should be something that you supplement with.

In general I find most people are concerned about calcium, zinc, iodine, and iron. Generally these do not need to be supplemented if you are getting in a rich diversity of nutrients from your diet. If you are concerned here are some plant foods rich in these four minerals:

Zinc - most beans (ex. aduki, garbanzo, white beans), seeds (ex. pumpkin, sesame, squash), whole grains (ex. whole wheat, quinoa, oats), and dried mushrooms

Iodine - sea vegetables (ex. dulse, nori, kelp)

Calcium - most leafy green vegetables (ex. kale, collards, arugula, broccoli) and beans

Iron - most leafy greens, legumes, and whole grains

Water and Other Drinks

In addition to beginning to eat more plant foods which are more water rich foods, it is important to drink enough water daily to stay hydrated and help all the fiber in your new diet move through your system effectively. Drinking at least 2 liters per day (or up to a gallon if you are very active or live in a warm climate) will ensure hydration. Some signs of dehydration can include: fatigue, lack of energy, irritability, rapid heart rate, excess hunger, and dry skin. Proper hydration is important for healthy skin and hair, and for the functioning of all your internal organs. If you are someone who initially does not enjoy the "chore" of drinking water, try creating a fruit infused water blend to help it taste more exciting. Try out these simple combinations:

Blueberries and Peaches (blueberries are are high in antioxidants, boost the immune system, and provide potential protection against cancer)

Strawberries and Mint (mint soothes the stomach and reduces inflammation)

Lemon and Lime (both are a natural detoxifiers, and aid with bloating and fluid retention)

Cucumber and Cantaloupe (cucumber cools, hydrates, reduces puffiness and bloating, and flushes toxins)

You can also add in green tea, white tea, or herbal teas (such as hibiscus, nettle, lemon balm, peppermint or other herbal teas of your choice). Drinking these teas provide you with a multitude of health benefits and are a great go-to for a pick me up in between or after meals.

Sweeteners?

When it comes to weight loss, the less sweeteners consumed the better. Sticking to fruit, or dates to sweeten naturally is truly the best choice. That being said, some of the recipes in this book do include maple syrup or monk fruit sweetener in them. These are acceptable more natural options to use on occasion, but if you want to omit or reduce them please feel free.

Salt?

In short, yes but I recommend using as little added sodium as necessary. When you use it, aim to add it to your plate at the table as opposed to cooking with it in a recipe. You will get a better bang for your buck and be able to taste it more while using less. Overtime your taste buds will evolve and you will get used to using less salt overall.

Caffeine and Alcohol?

There are many mixed opinions on both of these, but we know that overuse of either has addictive properties as well as attributes to more acid in the body. There is also a link between alcohol consumption and certain cancers. The choice is up to you, but also keep in mind if you are trying to lose weight alcohol and specialty coffees are high in calories, and may derail your weight loss efforts.

KITCHEN TOOLS

Blender: If you like sauces, dips, dressings or smoothies I encourage you to invest in a high speed blender like a Vitamix or a Blendtec. It will really make a difference in the quality and variety of what you can prepare. While these are significant investments, they will be used daily and are worth the cost over time.

Food Processor: Even a cheaper quality food processor will do and they are great for making things like hummus, salsa, and spreads.

Nonstick Pans: To cook without oil, a good nonstick pan makes all the difference. Look for ceramic titanium or cast iron and avoid teflon as it contains toxicities. Even having one high sided skillet or wok will be enough. You can use this for stir fries, scrambles, sauces, and even soups.

A Good Knife and Cutting Board: Trust me, you will be cutting and chopping a lot so these will be essential.

Rice Cooker or Slow Cooker: These are very affordable and helpful tools for prepping things like grains and beans ahead of time. They take the guesswork out of cooking grains and also allow you to slow cook things like beans, soups, stews, and oats overnight.

Clean Kitchen Environment

By this I mean that your pantry, fridge, and freezer are filled with high quality, nutrient rich foods that you can access to make delicious whole food meals. You will want to eliminate processed sugars, processed white flours, all oils and vegan margarines. High salt foods, and foods that are highly processed (bear little resemblance to their original state, do not spoil easily, have a long list of ingredients, are packaged or boxed, often found in the center of the grocery store). Remove all of these from your kitchen environment. If these foods are easily accessible they will be even more appealing once you have made up your mind to make positive changes in your health. So go ahead and clean up your pantry, fridge, and freezer getting rid of foods that may prove to be a pitfall. This will help set you up for success and not have temptations knocking at your door.

SECTION 2 -
WEIGHT LOSS FOUNDATIONS

Know your "Why"

Whenever you make a significant shift in your life, it's best to be prepared and really know the reasons why you are wanting to commit to changing. Perhaps you were given scary results at a doctors office, or you are trying to lose weight to improve the quality of your life. Maybe a friend or a movie has convinced you to make a change, or you are doing this for ethical reasons. All of these and more are worthy reasons to make a change. Whatever your reason, take full responsibility for your choice, embrace it and be accountable for your choice to do so. After a few weeks of eating this way your future self will thank you.

Eat According to Calorie Density

Not all calories are created equally and using calorie density to your benefit is a wonderful tool to help you feel satisfied while on your weight loss journey. Calorie density is simply a measure of how many calories are in a given weight of food, most often expressed as calories per pound. A food high in calorie density has a large number of calories in a small weight of food, whereas a food low in calorie density has much fewer calories in the same weight of food. Often times just reducing the amount of higher calorie density foods (for example, eliminating oil) from your diet will result in weight loss. Sticking to foods that are high in volume and lower in calorie density will be one of your greatest tools to lose weight (see **Calorie Density Chart p. 23**).

Plan Ahead for Success

Chose one day a week to make a shopping list, go to the grocery store, and prepare for the meals ahead of time that you will be having in the upcoming week. This can be the same day that you batch cook (preparing staples in large quantities for use throughout the week or to be frozen in serving-size containers for reheating). Batch cooking or batch preparation can include things like a large pot of whole grains, beans, a vegetable based soup, potatoes, dips, oil free dressings, nut milk, or even just pre-cutting some vegetables to get ready for the week of recipes ahead. Make these preparations last by making sure to use the batch items more than once through out the week and learn to love your leftovers to help stretch your budget and eat everything you have taken the time to prepare.

Utilize the Concept of "The First Course"

Think about starting each meal with a *First Course*. Your *First Course* will consist of fruits and vegetable. This is your "weight loss / medicine / multivitamin food." It could be a bowl of berries or other fruits before breakfast, a big salad with lunch, or a vegetable based soup before dinner. Make these a big portion.

Your *Second Course* will consist of highly satiating whole foods like whole grains, starchy vegetables or beans. This is your way to feel full so eat a large enough portion to feel satisfied.

While you don't want to completely eliminate the following, for weight loss you will only want to consume a small amount of more calorie dense foods like nuts, seeds, avocados, olives, dried fruit, and minimally processed foods (whole grain pastas, breads, nut milk, tofu, or animal foods if you are including them etc.) If you are already full and don't need these types of foods, don't eat them. If you do eat them, just keep your portions smaller. This is a great way to train yourself to be mindful of the foods you eat.

Exercise

Exercise can help ward off mild cognitive decline, boost the immune system, prevent and treat high blood pressure, improve mood and quality of sleep, not to mention aid in maintaining a healthy body weight and building muscle tone. I suggest trying to incorporate at least 30 - 60 minutes of exercise 3 - 6 times a week. If you are someone who does not currently exercise, please start slow. As you begin to feel the benefits of your new diet and exercise regime, feel free to add additional days, length of time, and intensity. Try out new forms of exercise that seem like fun and something you will stick with. From walking, to weight lifting, hiking, swimming, biking, or Pilates and Yoga. There are so many forms of exercise to try that will get your heart pumping and give you the mental clarity to take on goals and achieve what you would like to accomplish in your life.

Track your Weight Loss Before and After

I know if you are like me, it can be scary to jump on the scale after you know you have indulged a bit too much. But taking stock of your "before" is so important and a huge motivator to confront your habitual patterns with the food you eat and the weight loss goals you want to achieve. A few ways I recommend documenting this journey are:

Get your starting weight, and weigh yourself daily, weekly or bimonthly. Whatever way feels like it makes the most sense to you.

Get your starting measurements (upper arms, bust, under bust, waist, hips, thighs) and circle back to them 10 - 12 weeks in.

Take full body photos (they don't need to be shared with anyone, this is just for your documentation) front, side, and back on a weekly basis.

Journal

Keeping track of when you eat, how you are feeling, and why you are eating is important to locate yourself when it comes to eating for fuel (when you are truly hungry) versus eating that is driven by your emotions (ex. anger, boredom, sadness). This can also encompass tracking your calories if you choose, but it is not necessary. If you do choose to track your food, write down EXACTLY what you ate, including any snack, beverages, tastes, bites, or licks. How you felt before you ate, during and after. Write how you slept, how you felt as you woke up, any physical sensations like headaches, heartburn, digestive woes. Reassess weekly for self reflection and to make any necessary changes for the upcoming week.

It can be hard to face yourself initially, but once you begin to see progress, you will be so happy you decided to document your "before" to have something to compare your results to.

Calorie Density Chart

AVERAGE CALORIES PER POUND

100	300	400-600	750	1,200-1,800	2,500	2,800	4,000
NON STARCHY VEGETABLES	FRUIT	UCC (Unrefined Complex Carbohydrates)	AVOCADOS	RCC (Refined Complex Carbohydrates) and Diary	CHOCOLATE	NUTS	ALL OILS
		POTATOES				SEEDS	
		WHOLE GRAINS		ICE CREAM = 1,200		NUT BUTTERS	
		LEGUMES		BREAD = 1,400		TAHINI	
				CHESSE = 1,600			
				SUGAR = 1,800			

The foods in GREEN are WHOLE FOODS found in nature and contain vitamins, minerals, antioxidants, phytochemicals and micronutrients. They also contain fiber and water, which create bulk and increased satiety.

The foods in RED are processed foods not found in nature. They contain few to no micronutrients and little to no fiber or water. They contribute very little to satiety.

The foods in BLUE are healthful foods but are calorie dense and are best included in small amounts after weight loss is achieved.

For weight loss, weight management and optimum health:

EAT TO THE LEFT OF THE RED LINE.

SECTION 3 - EATING WHOLE 28 DAY MEAL PLAN

I have designed the 28 Day Meal Plan using the recipes found in Section 4 of this book. You can follow the meal plan exactly, or mix and match to suit your tastes and preferences. If you are short on time, you can always fall back on the "Basics" in the recipe sections to get you through healthfully without much time or preparation involved.

Eat Enough - So you feel satisfied, but not so much that you are over stuffed. Remember if you are following the meal plan specifically for weight loss, you want to utilize the concept of the "First Course" by adding a bowl of fresh fruit, a large salad, steamed veggies, or a vegetable based soup as your "First Course" with each meal. This is your "weight loss / medicine / multivitamin food." Make these big portions. I have added suggestions with each meal but feel free to mix it up to suit your daily preference. This will play a big key in eating according to Low Calorie Density while still maintaining a calorie deficit to lose weight.

Plan a Week of Meals in Advance - This might mean planning, and taking a few hours on the weekend (for example) to shop and prepare. If you plan on using the 28 Day Meal Plan as written, you can take a look at the upcoming weeks recipes and make a shopping list accordingly.

Batch Cook Each Week - Taking a few hours once a week to prepare your staples for the upcoming week will save you time in your day to day and help you stay on track with your weight loss goals.

I have included some ideas on what to prepare "on the weekend" for each week, but you can always take it a few steps further to ensure your success. Examples of what you might like to batch cook could be:

- A big pot of whole grains of choice

- A big pot of beans (or just use canned to save time)

- Soups

- Baked or steamed potatoes

- Hummus

- Tofu or Tempeh

- Blend up a jar of no oil salad dressing

- Washing, drying, or even cutting fruits and veggies

EATING WHOLE 28 DAY MEAL PLAN - WEEK 1

ON THE WEEKEND	MONDAY	TUESDAY	WEDNESDAY	
Make *Oil Free Hummus* (p.122) - make enough for a wrap and a dip per person	**BREAKFAST** *Basic Breakfast Bowl* (p.42)	**BREAKFAST** *Green Smoothie Bowl* (p.56)	**BREAKFAST** *Zucchini Oats* (p.52)	
Make *Fennel Bean Soup* (p.72) - make enough for at least 2 servings per person	**LUNCH** *Apple Citrus Salad* (p.90) and *Basic Wrap* (p.136) with *No Oil Hummus* (p.122)	**LUNCH** *Fennel Bean Soup* (p.72) with *Basic Big Salad* (p.96) (dressing of choice)	**LUNCH** *No Tuna Salad Sandwich* (p.140) with *Basic Big Salad* (p.96) (dressing of choice)	
Make *Granola* (p.44) - making a full batch will allow you to have enough for the entire 28 days	**DINNER** *Peanut Soba Noodles* (p.164)	**DINNER** *Mashed Potatoes with Mushroom Gravy* (p.160) and *Sauerkraut Salad* (p.88)	**DINNER** *Loaded Baked Potato* (p.186) with steamed veggies of choice	

THURSDAY	FRIDAY	SATURDAY	SUNDAY
BREAKFAST Omega-3 Blueberry Smoothie (p.38)	**BREAKFAST** Fresh Fruit with Granola (p.44)	**BREAKFAST** Whole Pancakes with fresh fruit (p.48)	**BREAKFAST** Tofu Scramble (p.54)
LUNCH Crispy Tofu Bowl with Plum Sauce (p.144)	**LUNCH** Basic Big Salad (p.96) (dressing of choice), leftover Fennel Bean Soup, and raw veggies of choice with leftover No Oil Hummus	**LUNCH** Any leftovers you have from the week, making sure to add extra veggies of choice	**LUNCH** Leftover Chili with Basic Big Salad (p.96)
DINNER Creamy Sun-dried Tomato Mushroom Pasta (p.180) with Basic Big Salad (p.96) (dressing of choice)	**DINNER** Alfredo Pizza (p.166) with Basic Big Salad (p.96) (dressing of choice)	**DINNER** Satisfying Chili (p.80) with brown rice and steamed veggies of choice	**DINNER** Hearty Lentil Loaf with Mashed Potatoes (p.172) and steamed veggies of choice

EATING WHOLE 28 DAY MEAL PLAN - WEEK 2

ON THE WEEKEND	MONDAY	TUESDAY	WEDNESDAY	
Cook *Cuban Black Beans* (p.82) - make enough for at least 3 servings per person	**BREAKFAST** *Steel Cut Oats with Caramelized Banana* (p.46)	**BREAKFAST** *Basic Smoothie* (p.40)	**BREAKFAST** *Fresh Fruit with Granola* (p.44) (you should still have this prepared from week 1)	
Make *Spilt Pea Soup* (p.62) - make enough for at least 2 servings per person	**LUNCH** Brown rice with *Cuban Black Beans* (p.82) and *Basic Big Salad* (p.96) (dressing of choice)	**LUNCH** *Spilt Pea Soup* (p.62) with *Jicama Wraps* (p.148)	**LUNCH** *Sweet Potato Miso Sushi* (p.176) with steamed organic edamame	
Cook brown rice - make enough for at least 4 servings per person. The "sushi rice" can be made from this as well on the day of.	**DINNER** *Roasted Butternut Squash Soup* (p.64) with steamed veggies of choice	**DINNER** *Pad Thai* (p.156)	**DINNER** *Chana Masala* (p.154) with brown rice and *Basic Big Salad* (p.96) (dressing of choice)	

THURSDAY	FRIDAY	SATURDAY	SUNDAY
BREAKFAST *Omega-3 Blueberry Smoothie* (p.38)	**BREAKFAST** *Basic Breakfast Bowl* (p.42)	**BREAKFAST** *Tofu Scramble* (p.54)	**BREAKFAST** *Whole Pancakes* (p.48) with *Blueberry Syrup* (p.51)
LUNCH *Smoked Tempeh Wrap* (p.150) with added fresh veggies	**LUNCH** *Spilt Pea Soup* with *Basic Bowl* (p.138)	**LUNCH** Any leftovers you have from the week, making sure to add extra veggies	**LUNCH** *Basic Big Salad* (p.96) (dressing of choice) with *Roasted Ranch Chickpeas* (p.132) and *Quick Tomato Soup* (p.170)
DINNER *Loaded Nacho Salad* (p.92) (use your precooked *Cuban Black Beans*)	**DINNER** *Creamy Tomato Basil Penne* (p.170) with *Basic Big Salad* (p.96) (dressing of choice)	**DINNER** *Sweet Potato Enchiladas* (p.182) (use your precooked *Cuban Black Beans*)	**DINNER** *Ramen Noodle Soup* (p.76)

EATING WHOLE 28 DAY MEAL PLAN - WEEK 3

ON THE WEEKEND	MONDAY	TUESDAY	WEDNESDAY	
Cook *Bean with "Bacon"* (p.84) - make enough for at least 2 servings per person	**BREAKFAST** *Zucchini Muffin* (p.194) with fresh fruit	**BREAKFAST** *Green Smoothie Bowl* (p.56)	**BREAKFAST** *Basic Smoothie* (p.40)	
Cook brown rice or quinoa - make enough for at least 2 servings per person	**LUNCH** *Pickled Gherkin Vegetable Soup* (p.74) with *Basic Big Salad* (p.96) (dressing of choice)	**LUNCH** *No Oil Fries* (p.175) with *Basic Big Salad* (p.96) (dressing of choice)	**LUNCH** *Bean with "Bacon"* (p.84) with brown rice and steamed veggies of choice	
Make *Pickled Gherkin Vegetable Soup* (p.74)- make enough for at least 2 servings per person *Bake Zucchini Muffins* (p.194) - one batch	**DINNER** *Satisfying Chili* (p.80) with brown rice and steamed veggies of choice	**DINNER** *Peanut Soba Noodles* (p.164)	**DINNER** *Creamy Sun-dried Tomato Mushroom Pasta* (p.180) with *Basic Big Salad* (p.96) (dressing of choice)	

THURSDAY	FRIDAY	SATURDAY	SUNDAY
BREAKFAST Steel Cut Oats with Caramelized Banana (p.46)	**BREAKFAST** Fresh fruit bowl with a sprinkle of chia seed or flaxseed (freshly ground)	**BREAKFAST** Tofu Scramble (p.54)	**BREAKFAST** Basic Smoothie (p.40)
LUNCH Pickled Gherkin Vegetable Soup with steamed veggies of choice	**LUNCH** Basic Bowl (p.138) with leftover Bean with "Bacon"	**LUNCH** Any leftovers you have from the week, making sure to add extra veggies	**LUNCH** Loaded Nacho Salad (p.92)
DINNER Leftover Satisfying Chili with No Oil Fries (p.175) and Basic Big Salad (p.96) (dressing of choice)	**DINNER** Alfredo Pizza (p.166) with Basic Big Salad (p.96) (dressing of choice)	**DINNER** Creamy Mushroom with Brown Rice Soup (p.66)	**DINNER** Basic Wrap (p.136) with added veggies of choice with homemade Tortilla Chips (p.95) and Staple Salsa (p.126)

EATING WHOLE 28 DAY MEAL PLAN - WEEK 4

ON THE WEEKEND	MONDAY	TUESDAY	WEDNESDAY	
Cook *Pinto Beans* (p.82) - make enough for at least 2 servings per person	**BREAKFAST** *Basic Breakfast Bowl* (p.42)	**BREAKFAST** *Basic Smoothie* (p.40)	**BREAKFAST** Fresh fruit bowl with a sprinkle of chia seed or flaxseed (freshly ground)	
Hearty Lentil Loaf (p.172) - make full loaf and reheat to serve	**LUNCH** *Ramen Noodle Soup* (p.76) with steamed organic edamame	**LUNCH** *Basic Bowl* (p.138) with extra steamed veggies and *All Purpose Fat Free Cheese Sauce* (p.118)	**LUNCH** *Loaded Baked Potato* (p.186) with *All Purpose Fat Free Cheese Sauce* (p.118)	
Make *All Purpose Fat Free Cheese Sauce* (p.118) - make enough for at least 2 serving per person	**DINNER** *Basic Wrap* (p.136) (use precooked pinto beans), add *Staple Salsa* (p.126) and *Guacamole* (p.124)	**DINNER** *Hearty Lentil Loaf* (p.172)	**DINNER** *Tofu Scramble* (p.54) with added steamed veggies of choice	

THURSDAY	FRIDAY	SATURDAY	SUNDAY
BREAKFAST *Omega-3 Blueberry Smoothie* (p.38)	**BREAKFAST** *Steel Cut Oats with Caramelized Banana* (p.46)	**BREAKFAST** *Whole Pancakes* (p.48) with fresh fruit	**BREAKFAST** *Tofu Scramble* (p.54)
LUNCH *Apple Citrus Salad* (p.90) with *Quick Tomato Soup* (p.70)	**LUNCH** *Smoked Tempeh Wrap* (p.150) with added veggies of choice	**LUNCH** Any leftovers you have from the week, making sure to add extra veggies	**LUNCH** *Quinoa Salad Bowl* (p.100) (use pinto beans)
DINNER *Mashed Potatoes And Mushroom Gravy* (p.160) with *Sauerkraut Salad* (p.88)	**DINNER** *Creamy Tomato Basil Penne* (p.170)	**DINNER** *Fennel Bean Soup* (p.72) with Basic Big Salad (p.96) (dressing of choice)	**DINNER** *Pad Thai* (p.156)

SECTION 4 - RECIPES

BREAKFAST
- Omega-3 Blueberry Smoothie
- Basic Smoothie
- Basic Breakfast Bowl
- Fresh Fruit with Granola
- Steel Cut Oats with Caramelized Banana
- Whole Pancakes
- Blueberry Syrup
- Zucchini Oats
- Tofu Scramble
- Green Smoothie Bowl

SOUPS AND BEANS
- Split Pea Soup
- Roasted Butternut Squash Soup
- Creamy Mushroom Soup with Brown Rice
- Quick Tomato Soup
- Fennel Bean Soup
- Pickle Gherkin Vegetable Soup
- Ramen Noodle Soup
- Satisfying Chili
- Cuban Black Beans or Pinto Beans
- Vegan Bean with "Bacon"

SALADS AND DRESSINGS
- Sauerkraut Salad
- Apple Citrus Salad
- Loaded Nacho Salad
- Basic Big Salad
- Quinoa Salad
- 4 Oil Free Salad Dressings
- Vegan Caesar Dressing
- Balsamic Vinaigrette
- Maple Mustard Dressing
- Tahini Ginger Dressing

DIPS, SPREADS, AND TOPPINGS
- Queso Dip
- All Purpose Fat Free Cheese Sauce
- Cashew Sour Cream
- No Oil Hummus
- Guacamole
- Staple Salsa
- Mango Salsa
- Roasted Ranch Chickpeas

WRAPS, SANDWICHES, BOWLS
- Basic Wrap
- Basic Bowl
- No Tuna Salad Sandwich
- Crispy Tofu Bowl
- Jicama Wrap
- Smoked Tempeh Wrap

MAIN DISHES
- Chana Masala
- Pad Thai
- Mashed Potatoes and Mushroom Gravy
- Peanut Soba Noodles
- Alfredo Pizza
- Creamy Tomato Basil Penne
- Hearty Lentil Loaf
- Sweet Potato Miso Sushi
- Creamy Sun-dried Tomato Mushroom Pasta
- Sweet Potato Enchiladas
- Loaded Baked Potato

DESSERTS AND WARM DRINKS

- Homemade Apple Sauce
- Zucchini Muffins
- Banana Bread
- Basic "Nice" Cream
- Chocolate Shake
- Golden Milk Latte
- Quick Hot Chocolate
- Chai Masala Mix & Chai Tea Latte

If you like the information you see in this cookbook, but need more guidance, I'd love to work with you one-on-one.

Learn More:
veganmichele.com/coaching

BREAKFAST

OMEGA-3 BLUEBERRY SMOOTHIE

Serves 1

- 1 frozen banana (peeled and in chunks)

- 1 cup frozen blueberries (wild if you can find them)

- 1 cup desired plant milk

- 1 tbsp chia seeds

- 1/2 tsp peanut or almond butter

- desired amount of kale or spinach (optional)

Add frozen banana, blueberries, peanut or almond butter, chia seeds, kale or spinach (optional), and plant milk to a high speed blender and blend on high until creamy and smooth. If it seems too thick, add more plant milk.

Serve immediately.

BASIC SMOOTHIE
Serves 1

Add desired ingredients to a high speed blender and blend on high until creamy and smooth.

Serve immediately.

- 1 cup plant milk or water

- 1 banana

- 1 cup fruit of your choice (berries, mango, pineapple, peach, etc.)

- a few handfuls of raw greens (kale, spinach, etc.)

- 1 tsp of seeds (chia, hemp, flax)

BASIC BREAKFAST BOWL

Serves 1

- 1/4 - 1/2 cup of dry oatmeal (I like steel cut oats)

- fruit of your choice (fresh or frozen)

- small amount of nut butter, or a sprinkling of seeds (hemp, chia, flax)

- sweeten with raisins or dates

- desired amount of plant milk

In a medium saucepan cook oats according to package directions.

Add plant milk as desired to reach a consistency you like. Once cooked, garnish with desired toppings and enjoy.

FRESH FRUIT WITH GRANOLA

Makes 3 - 4 cups

- 1 cup buckwheat groats

- 1 and 1/2 cups steel cut oats

- 1 - 2 tbsp coconut flakes

- 1 - 2 tbsp slivered raw almonds

- 1 tbsp chia seeds

- pinch of salt

- 1/2 cup maple syrup

- 3 dates (pitted, and soaked to soften if they are hard)

- 1 tbsp water

- 1 tsp vanilla

- 1/4 cup aquafaba (canned chickpea water)

- desired amount of fresh fruit

Preheat oven to 325 °F and line a baking sheet with parchment paper.

In a large bowl add the groats, oats, coconut flakes, almonds, chia seeds and a pinch of salt.

In a high speed blender add the maple syrup, vanilla and dates. Blend on high for 1 minute until smooth.

Add aquafaba (chickpea water) to a mixing bowl and using an electric whisk or mixer, whip into loose peaks. This can take up to 5 minutes.

Add the maple syrup mixture to the aquafaba and whisk or beat for another 30 seconds until combined.

Pour the liquid mixture over the dry ingredients bowl and fold to coat.

Spread the granola mixture evenly on to the parchment paper lined baking sheet and bake for 30 - 35 minutes, checking every 10 - 15 minutes to make sure it is not burning. Stir about half way in between the cooking time to ensure even baking.

Let the granola cool completely.

Store in an air tight glass container or jar for 2 - 3 weeks at room temperature. Store in the freezer up to 3 months.

Serve a small amount with a big bowl of fresh fruit, or serves well as a cereal with plant based milk.

STEEL CUT OATS WITH CARAMELIZED BANANAS

Serves 1

In a VERY hot non stick pan (key to caramelizing them without oil) place the sliced bananas face down and allow to cook 1 - 2 minutes. Flip over and cook for another 1 - 2 minutes until browned to your liking.

Cook desired amount of oats according to package directions.

Serve oats with the desired amount of caramelized bananas and enjoy. This combo works really well cooked ahead of time if need be. You can serve with a bit of plant milk if desired as well as fresh berries. No need for added sugar as the bananas make the oats so sweet.

- 1/4 - 1/2 cup of dry steel cut oats

- 1 very ripe spotty banana (peeled, cut in half, and sliced length wise so that all together you have 4 pieces of bananas)

Note: *Make sure you have very ripe bananas as the sugars in them are key to bringing out the sweetness.*

WHOLE PANCAKES
Makes 12 to 18 pancakes

If using an electric griddle, preheat it to 400 °F.

In a small bowl add the ground flaxseed and water to make a "flax egg" and let sit for 5 minutes.

If using homemade oat flour, blend it in a high speed blender until a flour consistency is achieved.

Then add all of the rest of the ingredients (omitting the fresh fruit) to the high speed blender. Blend on high for 1 minute until combined and smooth.

Pour batter by the 1/4 cup full onto the griddle/pan and heat 1 and 1/2 to 2 minutes per side. An indicator of when to flip is that they will form little bubbles.

Feel free to add your desired amount of berries/fruit to each pancake before flipping.

Allow to cool just a touch before serving, garnish with fresh fruit of your choice, or **Blueberry Syrup (p. 51)**, or a small amount of maple syrup if desired.

- 1 tbsp ground flaxseed + 2 and 1/2 tbsp water

- 1 tbsp maple syrup

- 1 ripe banana

- 1 cup plant milk + 2 tbsp

- 1 cup oat flour (just blend any oat in a high speed blender until it becomes flour)

- 1 tsp baking soda

- 1 tsp vanilla extract

- 1/4 tsp salt

- 1/2 tsp cinnamon

- fresh fruit of your choice for inside of the pancakes or for garnish

- non stick electric griddle or large non stick pan

BLUEBERRY SYRUP

Makes about 1 cup

- 2 cups fresh or frozen blueberries

- 1/4 cup freshly squeezed orange juice

- 2 tsp arrowroot powder

- 1 tbsp water

Place the berries and 1/4 cup juice in a small saucepan over medium heat. Cook for 5 - 10 minutes, until bubbling. Slightly smash some of the blueberries with the back of a fork. Let cool slightly.

In a small bowl, whisk together the arrowroot powder and water. Add the blueberry mixture. Let cool until slightly thickened and serve over pancakes.

Store in a glass container with a lid in the fridge for 3 - 5 days.

ZUCCHINI OATS
Serves 1

- 1/4 - 1/2 cup dry steel cut oats

- 1 small zucchini (peeled and grated)

- 1 ripe banana (sliced into coins)

- plant milk to taste

- desired toppings (almond butter, chia seeds, other fruit)

In a medium saucepan cook oats according to package directions adding in grated zucchini and banana until well combined and cooked through.

Add plant milk as desired to reach a consistency you like.

Once cooked, garnish with desired toppings and enjoy.

TOFU SCRAMBLE
Serves 4

- 14 oz. box extra firm organic tofu

- 1 medium sweet onion (chopped)

- 2 garlic cloves (chopped)

- 1/4 cup veggie broth for sautéing

- 2 tbsp soy sauce or tamari
(for gluten free option)

- 1 tsp dijon mustard

- 1/4 cup nutritional yeast (plus more for garnish)

- 1/2 tsp turmeric powder

- 1/2 tsp garlic salt

- 1 tbsp maple syrup

- 2 handfuls of spinach

- 14.5 oz. can of diced tomatoes (drained)

- salt and pepper to taste

Drain tofu of excess water. A technique you may want to try is wrapping the tofu in a few layers of paper towel then placing a cast iron pot on top to drain the water as much as possible. Once drained, crumble tofu into a mixing bowl in bite sized pieces resembling scrambled eggs.

In the mixing bowl with tofu, add soy sauce, mustard, nutritional yeast, turmeric, garlic salt, salt and pepper. Mix until combined well.

In a large frying pan add the veggie broth to sauté the onions and garlic. Sauté on medium high until the onions are softened and browned. About 5 - 7 minutes. Turn to a medium heat and add tofu mixture stirring frequently. Adding a bit of broth if it seems too dry. Cook for another 5 minutes.

Add in diced tomatoes and stir occasionally. Add maple syrup and spinach. Cook until spinach is slightly wilted. Give it a taste and add more salt, pepper, or nutritional yeast if desired.

Serve immediately and enjoy!

GREEN SMOOTHIE BOWL
Serves 1

- 2 frozen bananas

- 1/2 cup frozen pineapple

- small amount of plant milk (a splash up to a 1/4 cup just to get the mixture to blend)

- 2 coconut milk ice cubes (optional)

- 1 tsp or more of green powder (I like Daily Green Boost)

- desired toppings (I used shredded coconut, chia seeds, and freeze dried berries)

Place frozen fruit, plant milk, coconut milk ice cubes, and greens powder into a high speed blender.

Allow the frozen fruit and coconut milk ice cubes to defrost for about 3 - 5 minutes.

Then begin to blend on low. Using the tamper to aid in a low speed blend, gradually increase the speed until a thick creamy consistency is achieved.

You may need to add more plant milk, but do it conservatively as you don't want it to be too liquid-y.

HOW TO SOAK NUTS

Place the amount of nuts called for in the recipe into a small bowl. Fully cover with water. Soak anywhere from 2 - 3 hours, overnight in the refrigerator, or up to 24 hours. In general, harder nuts will take longer to soften. Try to squeeze in 20 minutes minimum, or just do a really good job rinsing them.

Note: *Soaking nuts minimizes the nutritional inhibitors and other toxic substances making the nutrients of the nuts more readily available for absorption.*

HOW TO MAKE NUT MILK
Makes 2 and 3/4 cups

Try almonds, cashews, walnuts or even hemp seeds.

• 1 cup nuts of choice (soaked and drained)

• 2 dates (pitted, optional)

• pinch of sea salt

• 3 cups water

Soak the nuts for at least 8 hours, then drain.

Combine nuts and 3 cups fresh water in a high speed blender, and blend until very smooth.

Strain through a nut milk bag, or cheese cloth.

Refrigerate in a glass container with lid up to 3 days.

SOUPS AND BEANS

SPLIT PEA SOUP

Serves 4

In a large soup pot add in the split peas, vegetable broth, and bay leaf. Allow to simmer on low heat slightly covered for 60 - 90 minutes.

After peas are almost tender, add the onion, carrot, sweet potato, thyme, pepper, 1 cup of water (add second cup if it needs more liquid). Simmer on low heat for another 15 - 20 minutes until vegetables are tender.

Turn off the heat completely, Cover and let stand for at least 10 minutes. Add fresh dill and serve.

- 1 cup dry green split peas (rinsed and drained)

- 8 cups vegetable broth

- 1 bay leaf

- 1 medium sweet onion (chopped)

- 1 carrot (chopped into rounds)

- 1 medium sweet potato (peeled and chopped)

- 1/2 tsp thyme

- 1/2 tsp black pepper

- 1 - 2 cups water

- 1 tbsp fresh dill (chopped)

ROASTED BUTTERNUT SQUASH SOUP

Serves 4

- 1 butternut squash (peeled, seeded, and chopped into 3/4 in. cubes)

- 1 large shallot (coarsely chopped)

- 4 garlic cloves (peeled but keep whole)

- 3 - 4 cups vegetable broth (I used Rapunzel Vegetable Bouillon with sea salt)

- Any additional spices you may enjoy (ex. paprika, ground pepper, cumin, thyme, sage, nutmeg)

Preheat oven to 400 °F.

On a parchment paper lined baking sheet place butternut squash, shallot, and garlic. Roast in the oven for 40 minutes or until the squash is fork tender. Allow to cool 10 - 15 minutes.

Place all roasted veggies and 3 cups vegetable broth in a Vitamix or high speed blender. Blend until smooth and steaming, about 4 - 5 minutes. Taste and see if you'd like to add the additional cup of broth or any additional spices, then serve.

Enjoy!

CREAMY MUSHROOM SOUP WITH BROWN RICE

Serves 4

- 3/4 cup brown rice (soaked for 30 minutes)

- 4 cups baby bella mushrooms (measure once sliced)

- 1 sweet onion (diced)

- 2 cloves garlic (minced)

- 4 cups vegetable broth + 1/2 cup vegetable broth for sautéing (I used Better Than Bouillon Vegetable Base)

- 1 tsp fresh thyme (finely chopped) + more for garnish

- 13.5 oz. can full fat coconut milk

- salt and pepper to taste

Rinse brown rice and soak in cold water in a small bowl for 30 minutes, then drain.

While rice is soaking, chop and prep vegetables. In a large soup pot add the 1/2 cup vegetable broth for sautéing over medium high heat. Once heated add in the mushrooms, onion, and garlic. Sauté for 15 minutes until the onion and mushrooms begin to cook down and brown. Add more broth if it is sticking. Stir consistently to evenly cook vegetables.

Once the vegetables are cooked, season with a bit of salt and pepper and the 1 tsp fresh thyme. Add in the 4 cups of vegetable broth, drained rice, coconut milk and stir until combined.

Bring the soup to a boil, then reduce to a simmer and cook slightly covered with lid for 20 minutes. After the 20 minute mark, remove the lid and continue to cook for another 15 - 20 minutes or longer until the rice is cooked. Add in an extra cup of broth if it seems too thick for you.

Remove the soup from heat. Add desired amount of salt and pepper. Let soup sit with a covered lid 5 - 10 minutes to thicken. Garnish with fresh thyme, salt, and pepper if desired.

Stores well in a covered glass container in the fridge for 3 - 4 days.

My favorite high speed blender is the Vitamix. Although it is an upfront investment, it will pay itself back over time. One of the reasons I enjoy it, is that it can make hot soups and dips. An easy staple soup in our house is my **Quick Tomato Soup** recipe on the following page.

QUICK TOMATO SOUP

Serves 2

- the juice of one orange

- 1/2 cup sweet cherry tomatoes

- 14.5 oz. can diced tomatoes

- 1/4 cup sun dried tomatoes (oil free)

- 1/2 large red bell pepper

- 2 cloves garlic

- 1 large carrot

- 1 green onion

- 1/2 cup raw cashews

- 1/4 tsp salt

- 1/4 tsp black pepper

- 1/4 tsp crushed red pepper (optional)

- 5 - 7 fresh basil leaves (1/2 for use in blender, 1/2 for garnish)

- nutritional yeast for garnish if desired

In a high speed blender add the orange juice, cherry tomatoes, diced tomatoes, sun dried tomatoes, red bell pepper, garlic, carrot, green onion, cashews, salt, black pepper, and crushed red pepper.

Blend on high for a few minutes until the soup is warm, and you can see some steam. Add in 1/2 of the basil leaves and pulse for about 10 seconds more.

Add more salt, black pepper, or crushed red pepper to taste. Pour in to bowls and garnish with remaining basil leaves. Sprinkle with crushed red pepper and nutritional yeast if desired. Enjoy this warm soup immediately.

Note: *If desired you can even use it as a creamy tomato sauce over cooked whole grain pasta or spiralized zucchini or cucumber.*

FENNEL BEAN SOUP

Serves 4

In a large soup pot, heat the 1/4 cup vegetable broth for sautéing. Add the fennel, onion and garlic. Cover and cook over low heat, stirring occasionally until softened, about 10 minutes. Add more broth if it is getting too dry. Uncover and cook over moderate heat, stirring occasionally, for another 10 minutes.

Add in the crushed red pepper, beans, 6 cups of broth and bring to a boil. Then reduce to a simmer over moderately low heat until the liquid is slightly reduced and the soup is chunky, about 30 minutes. Salt and pepper to taste.

Once you feel it is ready, turn off the heat and cover. Let it stand covered for at least 10 minutes before serving to allow flavors to intensify.

This is really easy to make, and so comforting! If you don't want to add the crushed red pepper, it still will taste great.

- 1/4 cup vegetable broth for sautéing (I used Better Than Bullion Vegetable Base)

- 1 large fennel bulb (chopped)

- 1 large onion (chopped)

- 2 garlic cloves (minced)

- 1/8 - 1/4 tsp crushed red pepper (optional, but totally recommended)

- 15.5 oz. can cannellini beans

- 6 cups vegetable broth (I used Rapunzel Vegetable Bouillon with sea salt

- salt and pepper to taste

PICKLED GHERKIN VEGETABLE SOUP

Serves 4

- 1/4 cup vegetable broth for sautéing

- 1 sweet onion (chopped)

- 3 cloves garlic (chopped) + 2 more cut in half length wise

- 8 cups vegetable broth (I used Rapunzel Vegetable Bouillon)

- 2 large russet or gold potatoes (peeled and chopped)

- 2 medium carrots (peeled and chopped)

- 2 celery ribs (chopped)

- 4 pieces whole all spice

- 1/2 tsp peppercorns

- 1 tsp thyme

- 1/2 tsp marjoram

- 5 pickled gherkins (chopped; Polish gherkins are the best if you can find them)

- 1/2 cup of the gherkin juice

- 1 tbsp fresh dill

- 1 tbsp fresh parsley

- salt and pepper to taste

In a large soup pot over medium heat, add 1/4 cup vegetable broth for sautéing the onions, chopped garlic and sauté until golden brown (7 - 10 minutes).

Add potatoes, carrots, celery, 8 cups of vegetable broth, all spice, the 2 garlic cloves cut in half, peppercorn, thyme and marjoram. Bring to a boil then turn down to a medium heat for about 20 - 25 minutes until vegetables are tender.

Add chopped gherkins and continue at a medium boil for 10 more minutes. Then add dill, parsley, gherkin juice and salt. Turn off the heat, cover and let stand for at least 10 minutes.

The longer it stands, the better it gets.

RAMEN NOODLE SOUP
Serves 4

- 6 cups vegetable broth (I used Better Than Bullion Vegetable Base)

- 6 small slices ginger root

- 1/4 - 1/2 jalapeño (cut lengthwise)

- 2 garlic cloves (crushed)

- 4 tbsp chickpea miso (I used Miso Master Organic)

- 4 oz. brown rice ramen noodles

- 6 crimini mushrooms (sliced)

- 4 green onions (all chopped, but separate the white from the green parts. Green parts are for garnish.)

- 2 cups green cabbage (grated)

- 1/2 tsp ginger root (grated)

- 1/2 tsp soy sauce or tamari (for gluten free option)

For Garnish

- jalapeño slices

- cilantro (chopped)

- mung bean bean sprouts

- green part of the green onion from above

- juice of 1 lime (or more if desired)

- Sriracha

In a large soup pot, heat the vegetable broth, sliced ginger, jalapeño cut lengthwise and garlic. Simmer gently for 10 minutes. Scoop out the ginger, jalapeño, garlic and discard. Turn off the heat, and then whisk in the miso until dissolved.

In a separate pot cook the ramen noodles according to the package directions, then drain.

In a small pan put a few tablespoons of water and water fry the mushrooms, cabbage, grated ginger, and white parts of the green onions for 3 minutes on medium heat stirring occasionally.

Add more water if it gets too dry. Add the soy sauce and cook for another minute.

Divide the noodles between 4 bowls. Pour the stock over the noodles, add the vegetables from other pan. Garnish with your desired amount of garnish from the list.

SATISFYING CHILI
Serves 6

- 1/4 cup vegetable broth for sautéing

- 3 garlic cloves (diced)

- 1/2 medium onion (diced)

- 1/2 red bell pepper (diced)

- 1 medium carrot (chopped)

- 1 medium celery rib (chopped)

- 14.5 oz. can diced tomatoes

- 15.5 oz. can kidney beans (drained)

- 1 cup red dry lentils

- 4 tbsp tomato paste

- 1/2 tsp smoked paprika

- 1/2 tsp cumin

- 1 chipotle pepper in adobo sauce

- salt and pepper to taste

- 3 cups water

- desired grain or potato for serving

For Garnish

Chose from any of the following: **Cashew Sour Cream (p. 120)**, fresh cilantro, lime, desired greens, green onions, avocado slices, red cabbage, jalapeño, or hot sauce.

If making a brown rice, barley, or potatoes get those started first.

Sauté garlic and onion with the 1/4 cup vegetable broth over medium heat for 5 minutes. Then add bell pepper, carrot, and celery and sauté 5 more minutes.

Add kidney beans, lentils, diced tomatoes, tomato paste, all spices, chipotle pepper, and water. Bring to boil, then simmer on low for 40 minutes or until everything tastes "done."

Add more spices or more water as needed.

Serve garnished with a dollop of Cashew Sour Cream, fresh cilantro, lime, greens, green onions, avocado slices, red cabbage, jalapeño or hot sauce if desired. Serve over brown rice, barley, sweet potatoes, or golden potatoes.

Feel free to store in the fridge or freezer in an air tight container. Will last in the fridge about a week, and can freeze for a long time and still taste good when thawed.

CUBAN BLACK BEANS or PINTO BEANS

Rinse the dry beans in a colander. Add them to a large pot and fill with enough water to cover the beans. Bring to a rapid boil for 5 minutes. Remove from heat and cover with a lid, let them stand while you sauté the veggies.

In a large frying pan on medium high heat add a bit of water or veggie broth, green bell pepper, garlic and onion; sauté until tender about 7 - 10 minutes.

Drain and rinse the beans once more, then add them to the slow cooker. Add the 6 cups of water, sautéed veggies, monk fruit sweetener, salt, vinegar, sherry, bay leaf, pepper, and cumin. Stir together then cover. Let this cook for 5 - 7 hours on a high to medium heat.

The beans are done when they are no longer hard and taste like, well, beans. You can add additional salt, sugar, pepper, or cumin at this time if desired.

Note: *To "refry" either bean in a healthy way, just place your desired amount into a high speed blender with a bit of the liquid from the slow cooker and blend until your desired consistency is achieved.*

This recipe works best with a slow cooker BUT it can be accomplished on the stove top, you just need to make sure you are home to keep an eye on the stove for 5 - 7 hours.

- 1 lb organic dry black beans OR organic pinto beans

- 6 cups water

- 1 large green bell pepper (diced)

- 4 medium garlic cloves (chopped)

- 1 medium sweet onion (chopped)

- 2 tbsp monk fruit sweetener

- 4 - 5 tsp salt (start with 4, add the last at the end if needed)

- 2 tbsp white vinegar

- 2 tbsp sherry wine

- 1 bay leaf

- 1/2 tsp black pepper

- 1/2 tsp cumin

VEGAN BEAN WITH BACON

Serves 4 - 6

- 1/4 cup vegetable broth for sautéing

- 2 cups dry great northern beans

- 1/2 medium yellow onion (diced)

- 1 medium carrot (diced)

- 1/2 of a celery rib (diced)

- 4 cups vegetable broth (I used Rapunzel vegetable bouillon cubes)

- 1/4 tsp liquid smoke

- salt as desired

Rinse the dry beans in a colander. In a medium sauce pan add the dry great northern beans and enough water to cover them. Bring to a rapid boil for 5 minutes. Remove from heat and cover with a lid, let them stand while you sauté the veggies. Then drain and rinse the beans once more.

In a large frying pan, add the 1/4 cup vegetable broth to fry the onion, carrot, and celery. Sauté and stir occasionally until softened for 3 - 5 minutes over medium heat. Then turn off and set aside.

In a slow cooker add the vegetable broth, liquid smoke, great northern beans, and the vegetables from the frying pan. Cook on high for 3 - 5 hours or until beans are cooked to desired tenderness. Add salt to taste.

Serve alone or over brown rice.

SALADS & DRESSINGS

SAUERKRAUT SALAD

Serves 4

Put all ingredients in a medium mixing bowl and stir until combined. Add more salt if desired.

Refrigerate covered to chill until ready to eat.

Stores well in a covered glass container in the fridge for 3 - 4 days.

- 16 oz. fresh sauerkraut

- 1 medium green apple (cored, peeled, and grated)

- 2 large carrots (peeled and grated)

- 1/3 cup sweet onion (measure when diced)

- 1/4 tsp salt

- 1/2 tsp black pepper

- 1/2 tsp monk fruit sweetener

APPLE CITRUS SALAD
Serves 4

- 1 small shallot (finely chopped)

- 1 tbsp fresh squeezed lemon juice

- 1 tbsp fresh squeezed lime juice

- 2 tsp maple syrup

- 1 tsp dijon mustard

- 1 small handful raw walnuts

- 1 large head boston lettuce (torn)

- 3 large handfuls of arugula

- 1 large green apple (thinly sliced)

- salt and pepper to taste

In a jar with a lid, add the shallot, lemon juice, lime juice, maple syrup, dijon mustard, salt and pepper. Close the lid and shake until combined.

In a large salad bowl add the lettuce, arugula, walnuts, and green apple.

Pour the dressing over the salad and toss.

LOADED NACHO SALAD
Adjustable serving

Choose your desired amounts of salad ingredients from this list and enjoy this as a large salad.

You can also add in some **Maple Mustard Vinaigrette (p. 108)** if you would like some extra fat free flavor.

- desired amount of **Homemade Corn Tortilla Chips (p. 95)**

- 1 - 2 tbsp **Queso Dip (p. 116)**

- **Mango Salsa (p. 130)** or **Staple Salsa (p. 126)**

- desired amount of cooked brown rice or baked sweet potatoes

- carrot (grated)

- red cabbage (grated)

- cucumber (chopped)

- mixed greens of choice

- kale

- spinach

- 1/4 of an avocado (sliced, diced, or mashed)

- desired amount of black or pinto beans

- fresh corn

- lime juice

HOW TO MAKE HOMEMADE CORN TORTILLA CHIPS

- 6 - 8 organic or non GMO corn tortillas

- sea salt (desired amount)

- lime juice (squeeze from 1/2 to a full lime)

Preheat oven to 450°F. Cut the tortillas into desired "chip" shapes. Place them on a parchment paper lined baking sheet in one layer, preferably not stacked on top of one another.

Spritz with squeezes of lime juice and sprinkle desired amount of sea salt making sure to get all the chips covered with lime juice and salt.

Bake for 10 - 15 minutes. If they are still bendable, bake for a few minutes longer watching carefully so as not to burn them.

BASIC BIG SALAD
Adjustable serving

The sky is the limit when it comes to building your Basic Big Salad. Try to incorporate 1 - 2 large salads the size of your head daily. Below are some suggestions of what to put in the salad, but make it your own. This will help you get in more raw, fresh vegetables, vitamins, antioxidants, minerals, fiber, quality carbs, proteins, and fats. Using these steps will help you build a large salad that is fulfilling and will help you stay on track with weight loss and optimal digestion.

Greens - kale, lettuce of your choice, arugula, spinach, mixed greens, endive, fresh herbs like cilantro, parsley, dill, basil etc.

Crunch - grated red or green cabbage, carrot, beets, broccoli, snap peas, cucumber

Savory - white onion, red onion, green onion, leeks, chives, garlic, roasted vegetables like brussels sprouts, carrots, corn etc.

Acid - balsamic vinegar, apple cider vinegar, red wine vinegar, rice vinegar, lemon, lime, citrus

Sweet - maple syrup, fresh fruit like berries, mango, pineapple dried fruit like dried cranberry, raisins, dates, prunes, fresh orange juice

Salty - rock salt, sea salt, nutritional yeast, nori, dulse, wakame seaweeds

Saucy - creamy dressings made with a small amount of nuts, seeds, avocado, or tahini. Add plenty of dried spices like turmeric, oregano, basil, cumin, paprika, red pepper flakes, cayenne pepper

If you are having it as a meal, then add some of the following as well:

Specialty - adding some leftovers can transform your salad into a meal. Things like leftover veggies, pasta, the possibilities are endless

Starches - grains like brown rice, farro, millet, quinoa, barley, potatoes, sweet potatoes

Beans and Legumes - black beans, kidney beans, great northern beans, pinto beans, chickpeas, lentils, tofu, tempeh, edamame, green peas etc.

Note: *Chopping greens very small, and shredding or grating the "crunch" ingredients will help you get in more volume and improve overall taste.*

QUINOA SALAD
Serves 4

- 1 cup quinoa

- 2 cups veggie broth (I used Better Than Bouillon Vegetable Base)

- 1 cup drained black beans or pinto beans (canned or homemade)

- 1/2 cup organic sweet corn (fresh or thawed from frozen)

- 1 large tomato (diced)

- 1/4 of an avocado (sliced for serving)

- desired amount of lettuce of your choice (for serving)

- green onions (chopped for garnish)

- **Mango Salsa (p. 130)**

Dressing

- 1/4 cup cilantro (finely chopped)

- 3 tbsp fresh lime juice

- 1/4 tsp cumin

- 1/4 tsp smoked paprika

- 1/4 tsp garlic salt

- 1 tsp maple syrup

In a medium saucepan bring the quinoa and veggie broth to a boil. Reduce heat to low, cover and let simmer on low for 20 minutes or until all the water is almost absorbed. Turn off heat and let sit for 5 minutes.

In the meantime make the dressing. Add all ingredients to a small glass jar, put lid on and shake vigorously until combined.

Once cooked, transfer the quinoa to a bowl to cool a bit (about 10 minutes).

Once slightly cooled, combine the quinoa, beans, corn, and tomato. Mix until combined and then pour dressing on, mixing until combined again. I really like this warm, but if you'd like to put it in the fridge at this point, you can serve it cold too.

Prep each plate by laying down a bed of your desired lettuce, and desired amount of quinoa salad. Garnish with sliced avocado, desired green onion and Mango Salsa.

4 OIL FREE SALAD DRESSINGS

Enough for a big salad each

- 1 garlic clove (crushed)

- 1 tbsp tahini

- 1 tbsp nutritional yeast

- 1 tbsp lemon juice

- 2 tbsp soy sauce or tamari (for gluten free option)

- water to thin as desired

- 2 tbsp lime juice

- 1 tbsp tahini

- 1 tsp maple syrup

- 1 garlic clove (crushed)

- water to thin as desired

- salt and pepper to taste

For all Dressings: Place ingredients into a small glass jar with lid and shake until well combined. Feel free to double any of these for easy access throughout the day or week. All keep in the fridge for 3 - 5 days.

- 2 tbsp rice vinegar

- 1 tsp dijon mustard

- 1 garlic clove (crushed)

- 1 tsp maple syrup

- salt and pepper to taste

- 2 tbsp rice vinegar

- 1 tsp maple syrup

- 1/8 tsp garlic salt

- 1/8 tsp paprika

- 1/8 tsp mustard

- salt and pepper to taste

For all Dressings: Place ingredients into a small glass jar with lid and shake until well combined. Feel free to double any of these for easy access throughout the day or week. All keep in the fridge for 3 - 5 days.

VEGAN CAESAR DRESSING

Makes 1 cup

- 1/4 cup raw cashews (soaked and drained)

- 1/4 cup water

- 1 clove garlic

- 1 and 1/2 tbsp lemon juice

- 1 tsp dijon mustard

- 1 tsp capers (drained)

- 1/2 tsp soy sauce or tamari (for gluten free option)

- 1 tbsp nutritional yeast

- salt and pepper to taste

Add all dressing ingredients to a high speed blender, and blend on high until smooth. Serve over desired salad ingredients.

Feel free to double this for easy access throughout the week. Keeps in the fridge for 3 - 5 days.

BALSAMIC VINAIGRETTE

Enough for a big salad

Place all ingredients into a small glass jar with lid and shake until well combined. Feel free to double this for easy access throughout the day or week. Keeps in the fridge for 3 - 5 days.

- 3 tbsp high quality balsamic vinegar

- 1 tbsp maple syrup

- 1 tbsp dijon mustard

- 1 garlic clove (crushed)

- salt, freshly ground black pepper, and nutritional yeast to taste

MAPLE MUSTARD DRESSING

Enough for a big salad

- 2 tbsp dijon mustard

- 1 tbsp maple syrup

- 1 tbsp lemon juice

- 1 tbsp rice vinegar

- 1 tbsp water

- salt and pepper to taste

Place all ingredients in a small glass jar with a lid and shake vigorously until combined. Pour desired amount over your preferred raw, steamed, or cooked vegetables. Keeps well in the fridge in a covered glass container for 3 - 5 days.

TAHINI GINGER DRESSING

Serves 2

Toss all ingredients into a high speed blender and blend on high for 1 - 2 minutes until smooth. Eat with desired greens and vegetables.

Stores well in a glass jar with a lid in the refrigerator for up to 1 week.

- 2 tbsp tahini

- 2 tbsp apple cider vinegar

- 2 tbsp soy sauce or tamari (for gluten free option)

- 2 tbsp lemon juice, adding more if needed

- 2 cloves garlic (crushed)

- 1 tsp fresh ginger (about 1/4 size of your pinky finger)

- 2 tbsp water to create your desired thickness, adding more if needed

- black pepper to taste

HOW TO MAKE NO OIL SALAD DRESSING

- 1 - 2 tbsp chopped nuts, such as walnuts, cashews, almonds, or pecans

- 1/4 cup chopped fresh fruit, such as plums, peaches, blueberries, or strawberries

- 1/4 cup unsweetened plant milk

- 1 tbsp lemon or lime juice (or vinegar)

- salt and pepper to taste

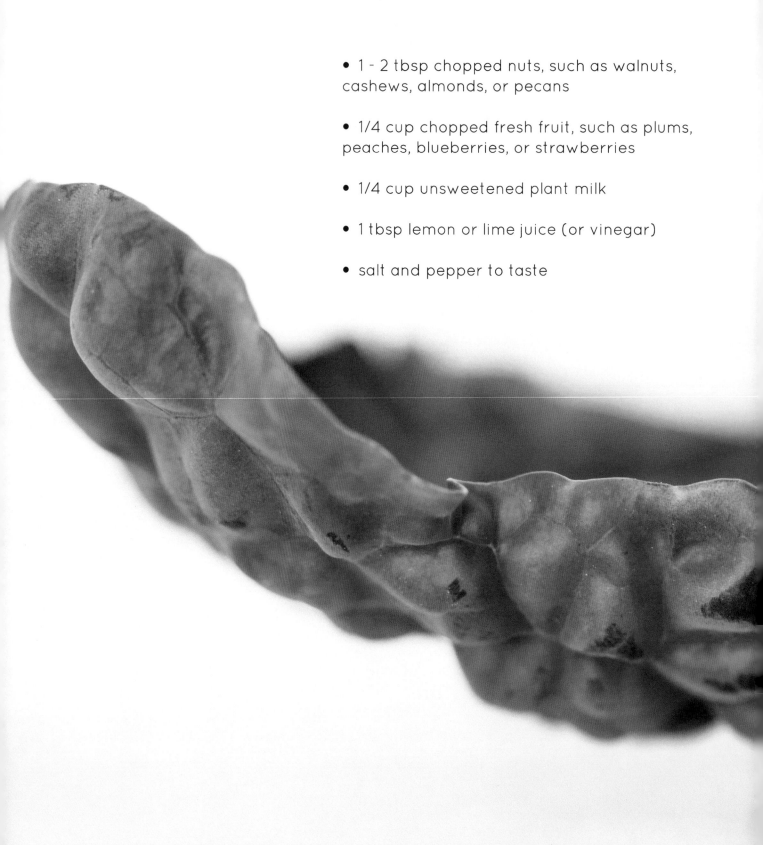

Toss all ingredients into a high speed blender and blend on high for 1 - 2 minutes until smooth. Eat with desired greens and vegetables. Stores well in a glass jar with a lid in the refrigerator for up to one week.

QUESO DIP
Makes 2 cups

- 1 and 1/2 cups raw cashews (soaked and drained)

- 3 tbsp nutritional yeast

- 1/2 tsp sea salt

- 1/4 tsp garlic salt

- 1/2 tsp cumin

- 1/2 tsp smoked paprika

- 1 cup of hot water

Place all ingredients into a high speed blender and blend on high until slightly warmed and steamy (around 1 - 2 minutes).

Stores well in a glass container with lid in the fridge for about 5 days.

ALL PURPOSE FAT FREE CHEESE SAUCE

Makes 4 cups

Boil carrots and potatoes in a medium sauce pan for 10 minutes or until fork tender. Drain.

Add all ingredients into a high speed blender and blend on high until very smooth. Taste and adjust seasoning as desired. Stores well in a glass container with lid in the fridge for about 5 days.

Note: *If you want to add a little bit of fat to this, swap out the 1/4 cup white kidney beans with a 1/4 cup raw cashews.*

- 1/4 cup carrots (chopped)

- 1 and 1/2 cups gold potatoes (peeled and chopped)

- 1/4 cup white kidney beans

- 1/2 cup water

- 2 tbsp nutritional yeast

- 1 tsp garlic salt

- 1/4 tsp salt

- 1/2 tsp lemon juice

CASHEW SOUR CREAM

Makes 1 cup

- 1 cup raw cashews (soaked and drained)

- 1/2 cup water

- 3 - 4 tbsp fresh lemon juice

- salt to taste

Blend everything in a high speed blender until creamy and steamy. About 3 - 4 minutes.

Stores well in a glass container with lid in the fridge for about 5 days.

NO OIL HUMMUS

Serves 4

Add all ingredients to a food processor and process until well combined and smooth. Stopping to taste and adding more lemon juice or water if needed to suit your desired taste and consistency.

Add salt and garlic salt to taste.

- 15.5 oz. can garbanzo beans (drained and rinsed)

- 3 tbsp lemon juice

- 1 garlic clove

- 4 tbsp tahini

- 2 - 3 tbsp water

- salt and garlic salt to taste

GUACAMOLE
Serves 4

- 3 ripe avocados (reserve 1 pit)

- juice of 1 and 1/2 - 2 limes

- 1 small tomato (chopped)

- 1/4 cup sweet onion (chopped)

- 2 garlic cloves (crushed)

- 1/4 of a jalapeño (diced)

- salt and pepper to taste

In a medium bowl scoop out all of the avocado (reserve one of the pits). Using a fork, mash the avocados coarsely.

Add in all the rest of the ingredients and stir until combined.

To slow browning of the guacamole, put the reserved pit back in, it really does help.

It's best to eat this the same day you make it, but it will last in a glass container with a lid in the fridge till the next day if need be.

STAPLE SALSA
Serves 4

Place all ingredients into a food processor and pulse to desired thickness. I like my salsa chunky so I pulse for a short time. Scrape the sides down, add more salt, cilantro, or lime to taste and pulse again.

This keeps well in a glass container with a lid refrigerated for 3 days.

- 1/4 of a small red onion

- 8 oz. fresh cherry tomatoes (quartered)

- 2 small tomatillos (quartered)

- 1 medium jalapeño (1/2 for medium, 1/4 for mild)

- 2 medium garlic cloves

- 1/4 cup cilantro coarsely chopped (more if desired)

- juice of one lime (or more if preferred)

- 1/2 red bell pepper (seeds and stem removed)

- 2 tbsp tomato paste

- salt to taste

Cilantro is a powerful herb that has anti-inflammatory and anti-bacterial properties. It helps prevent gas and bloating, and detoxes heavy metals.

MANGO SALSA
Serves 4

- 1/2 cup fresh mango (diced)

- 1/4 cup fresh corn

- 1/4 cup red onion (diced)

- 1/2 cup cilantro (finely chopped)

- 1 large tomato (diced)

- 1/4 - 1/2 jalapeño (diced)

- 1 large garlic clove (crushed)

- 1/4 tsp sea salt

- 3 tbsp fresh lime juice

Place all ingredients into a medium mixing bowl and stir until combined.

Store in a glass container with lid in the fridge for 2 - 3 days, but best when eaten fresh.

ROASTED RANCH CHICKPEAS

Makes about 2 cups

Preheat oven to 400°F.

Drain and rinse the chickpeas. Spread onto a paper towel to let air dry for 15 minutes.

In a medium mixing bowl add the apple cider vinegar, garlic powder, dill, parsley, salt, and pepper. Then add in the chickpeas and stir until combined well.

On a parchment paper lined baking sheet spread the chickpeas evenly. Bake for 30 - 45 minutes checking every 15 minutes to ensure even baking and browning.

Once baked to your liking, turn OFF the oven and leave the chickpeas inside for 10 - 15 minutes with the oven door cracked open to ensure maximum crispiness.

Take them out of the oven, and eat or allow to cool for another 10 minutes.

Store them in a glass container with air tight lid. Great for a snack, or on top of a big salad.

- 15.5 oz. can of garbanzo (drained and rinsed)

- 1 tbsp apple cider vinegar

- 1/2 tsp garlic powder

- 1 tsp dried or fresh dill (if using fresh, finely chopped)

- 1 tsp dried or fresh parsley (if using fresh, finely chopped)

- 1/2 tsp salt

- 1/4 tsp black pepper

WRAPS, SANDWICHES, BOWLS

BASIC WRAP
Serves 1

- whole grain wrap

- bean spread / hummus / beans of your choice

- few handfuls of greens (arugula, spinach, romaine, spring mix, etc.)

- cooked grains or potatoes of your choice

- raw veggies (carrot, zucchini, cabbage, cucumber, radish, tomato, peppers, anything you like)

- condiment (salsa, mustard, sriracha, oil free dressing)

Place desired ingredients into wrap. Roll it up and eat.

BASIC BOWL

Place desired ingredients into a bowl, and enjoy.

• raw or cooked greens (spinach, romaine, spring mix, kale, brussels sprouts, asparagus, broccoli, green beans, etc.)

• beans of choice

• grains of choice

• fresh herbs of choice

• sauce or condiment of choice (cashew sour cream, hot sauce, soy sauce, oil free dressing, etc.)

NO TUNA SALAD SANDWICH

Makes 2 large sandwiches, or 4 smaller sandwiches

- 15.5 oz. can garbanzo (rinsed and drained)

- 1/4 cup red onion (diced)

- 1/4 cup celery rib (diced)

- 1/4 cup gherkins (I used Polish)

- 1 tsp capers (drained and loosely chopped)

- 1 tsp dijon or spicy brown mustard

- 1 tbsp apple cider vinegar

- 2 tbsp vegan mayonnaise or mashed avocado

- 1/8 tsp soy sauce or tamari (for a gluten free option)

- 1 tsp maple syrup

- freshly cracked salt and pepper to taste

- fresh or dried dill to taste

For Serving

- desired amount of sliced whole grain bread for sandwich

- lettuce or greens of your choice

- tomato (sliced)

- sprouts

- hot banana peppers (sliced)

- carrot sticks for extra dipping (optional)

Place the garbanzo in a large mixing bowl and mash with a potato masher or fork.

Add the red onion, celery, gherkins, and capers to the garbanzo mixture and incorporate. Next add in the mustard, apple cider vinegar, vegan mayo / avocado, soy sauce, maple syrup, salt, pepper and dill. Mix until combined well. Taste and adjust seasoning as needed.

Toast bread if desired, and chop up desired veggies for serving (lettuce, tomato, sprouts, peppers etc.)

Assemble the sandwich using all of the above ingredients, and repeat for additional sandwiches.

HOW TO COOK RICE

Use 1 cup rice to 3 cups water. Put rice and water into a medium pot and bring to a boil over medium high heat. Reduce heat to medium low, cover pot, and simmer just until liquid is completely absorbed and rice is tender, about 40 minutes. No peeking until then; valuable steam escapes.

Set covered pot off the heat 10 minutes, then uncover and fluff rice with a fork. For perfect rice every time, you might consider investing in a rice cooker.

CRISPY TOFU BOWL WITH PLUM SAUCE

Serves 2

- 14 oz. extra firm tofu (pressed, drained, and cubed)

- steamed veggies of choice (I used broccoli and some frozen mixed veggies)

- pre-cooked brown rice or whole grain of your choice

Garnish

- sliced avocado

- sauerkraut or kimchi

- 1 green onion (chopped)

Marinade

- 4 tbsp soy sauce or tamari (for gluten free option)

- 2 tbsp rice vinegar

- 2 tbsp cornstarch

Plum Sauce

- 2 cloves garlic (minced)

- 1 inch ginger root (minced)

- 1/2 cup maple syrup

- 1/2 tsp chili flakes (optional)

- 4 tbsp tomato paste

- 6 tbsp soy sauce or tamari

- 2 tbsp rice vinegar

- 4 tsp arrowroot powder

- a few drops hot sauce if desired

Drain the tofu, wrap in a tea towel and place under something heavy like a cast iron pot to drain as much excess water out as possible.

In a medium mixing bowl make marinade for the crispy tofu, add tofu and coat. Set aside to marinate for at least 30 minutes.

If using an air fryer, place tofu on rack and bake for 10 - 15 minutes until slightly crispy at 400°F.

If using an oven, preheat to 400°F and place the tofu on a parchment paper lined baking sheet and bake for 10 - 15 minutes until slightly crispy.

While the tofu is baking, steam desired veggies and make the plum sauce. To make the plum sauce add all the plum sauce ingredients into a medium mixing bowl and combine until smooth.

In a wok or large frying pan add the sauce, the crispy tofu and coat. Warm for 1 - 3 minutes on a medium high heat until warm and a bit sticky in consistency.

Assemble bowls with desired amount of brown rice, steamed veggies, tofu and desired garnish.

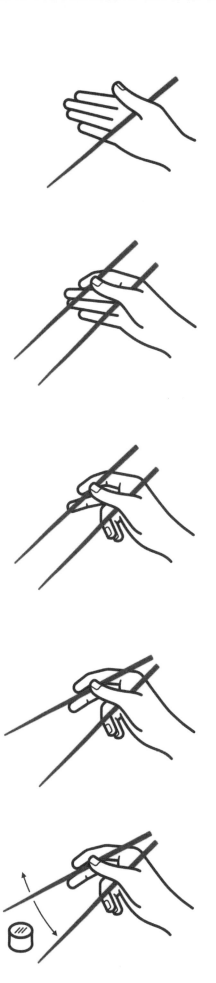

JICAMA WRAPS

Serves 4

- 1/2 cup vegetable broth

- 1 onion (chopped)

- 4 - 5 cloves garlic (minced)

- 1 jalapeño (diced)

- 2 and 1/2 cups fresh tomatoes (chopped) OR 14.5 oz. can diced tomatoes (drained)

- 1/2 cup fresh cilantro (chopped)

- 3 - 4 cups fresh spinach

- 4 cups small red or baby potatoes (steamed with skin on and cubed)

- 15 oz. can of black beans (drained)

- 1 tsp smoked paprika

- 1/4 tsp turmeric powder

- salt, freshly ground pepper, and hot sauce as desired

- Jicama wraps

- handful of microgreens for garnish

Steam potatoes, if you do not have them pre-steamed already.

In a large frying pan sauté the onion, garlic and jalapeño 3 - 5 minutes or until softened with the vegetable broth. Add tomatoes, cilantro, desired amount of freshly ground pepper and cook 10 - 15 minutes.

Add the can of beans, and potatoes to the pan, mix well. Add smoked paprika, turmeric, and desired salt and continue to cook over a medium heat for a few minutes until warmed. Add in the spinach and stir until wilted and combined.

Taste and add your desired salt, pepper, and / or hot sauce. Serve alone or inside of Jicama wraps as little tacos. Garnish with more cilantro, jalapeño, or vegetables of your choice.

Note: *Jicama wraps can be eaten raw, or steamed. To steam place desired amount of jicama wraps in a steam basket covered and steam 2 - 4 minutes.*

SMOKED TEMPEH WRAP

Serves 1

Slice the tempeh block into very thin slices (about a 1/4 inch thick).

In a small mixing bowl, add the soy sauce, liquid smoke, maple syrup, and garlic salt. Place the tempeh slices into the marinade and let it sit for 30 minutes.

If using an air fryer, place smoked tempeh onto the air fryer tray and bake at 400°F for 10 - 15 minutes or until crispy. Reserve remaining marinade sauce.

If using the oven, place your tempeh on baking sheet lined with parchment paper and bake at 400°F for 10 - 15 minutes or until crispy. Reserve remaining marinade sauce.

While the tempeh is baking, add remaining marinade sauce to a medium frying pan with about a 1/4 cup of water and heat over medium heat. Add in your vegetables (in my example: broccoli, mushrooms, bell peppers and green onions). Sauté for 3 minutes, then turn off the heat and cover allowing it to steam until softened (about 5 minutes).

Warm your wrap and assemble in this order: hummus, then steamed veggies, arugula, cabbage, desired amount of smoked tempeh. Wrap like a burrito and serve with hot sauce if desired. You will most likely have leftover tempeh.

It stores well in a glass container with lid for up to 5 days.

- 1 sprouted grain tortilla (I used an Ezekiel wrap)

- 1 package tempeh (very thinly sliced)

- 2 tbsp soy sauce

- 1/4 tsp liquid smoke

- 2 tbsp maple syrup

- 1/2 tsp garlic salt

- veggies of choice (I used broccoli, mushrooms, bell peppers and green onions)

- handful of greens (I used arugula)

- handful red cabbage (chopped)

- hot sauce if desired

- 2 tbsp **No Oil Hummus (p. 122)**

MAIN DISHES

CHANA MASALA

Serves 2

Heat a non stick frying pan over medium heat and add all of the ingredients (chickpeas, diced tomatoes, tomato paste, and all seasonings). Stir until combined and simmer on a medium low heat for 10 - 15 minutes stirring occasionally. Cooking less time if you prefer it more sauce like and more time if you prefer it on the dryer side. Taste and adjust seasoning.

Serve over potatoes, brown rice or another whole grain of choice. Enjoy this quick flavorful dish.

- 15.5 oz. can garbanzo (drained)

- 14.5 oz can diced tomatoes (slightly drained)

- 6 oz. can tomato paste

- 1 tsp fresh ginger (grated)

- 3 garlic cloves (minced)

- 1 tsp garlic salt

- 1/4 tsp turmeric powder

- 1/2 tsp curry powder

- 1/2 tsp cumin

- salt to taste

- 14 oz. rice noodles

- 8 cloves garlic (chopped)

- 2 red or orange bell pepper (remove stem, seeds, and slice)

- 8 green onions (chopped, white and green parts separated)

- 2 medium carrots (grated)

Pad Thai Sauce

- 1 and 1/3 cups vegetable broth (I used Better Than Bouillon Vegetable Base)

- 6 tbsp monk fruit sweetener or coconut sugar

- 4 tbsp soy sauce or tamari (for gluten free option)

- 1 tbsp Sriracha

Slurry

- 2 tbsp tapioca or arrowroot flour + 6 tbsp vegetable broth

Garnish

- 1 - 2 cups mung bean sprouts

- juice of 1/2 a lime (plus more for serving)

- desired cilantro (chopped)

- 1/3 - 2/3 cups dry roasted peanuts (chopped or crushed)

- 1/4 - 1/2 jalapeño (sliced for garnish)

Wash and prep veggies (garlic, bell pepper, green onions, carrot). When you chop the green onion make sure to separate the white and green parts.

Heat a large non stick pan or wok until hot, then add garlic and white portion of the green onions. Sauté stirring constantly over medium heat until browned for about 3 minutes.

Add in the bell pepper and carrot for about 5 more minutes stirring often. Add a bit of water if the veggies are sticking.

Make the Pad Thai Sauce by combining the vegetable broth, sugar, soy sauce, and Sriracha in a small bowl. Pour into the wok, combine and bring to a simmer.

As the sauce cooks, start the noodles and cook according to package directions. Drain and set aside.

In a small bowl mix together the slurry ingredients. Pour the slurry into the the wok. Mix and let it simmer until the sauce begins to thicken. Once thickened, add in the bean sprouts, green portion of the green onions, cooked noodles, lime juice, and peanuts.

Assemble bowls and garnish with more bean sprouts, lime, cilantro, peanuts, and jalapeño slices. Dig in, and enjoy!

MASHED POTATOES AND MUSHROOM GRAVY

Serves 4

Mashed Potatoes

- 3 lbs golden potatoes (peeled and quartered)

- 2 tbsp fresh thyme (optional)

- salt to taste

Mushroom Gravy

- 1/2 cup vegetable broth + a 1/4 cup for sautéing

- 1/2 cup sweet onion (diced)

- 2 garlic cloves (minced)

- 1/2 medium carrot (peeled and finely diced)

- 4 oz. mushrooms, I used baby bella mushrooms (thinly sliced)

- 1/2 tsp fresh thyme (finely chopped)

- 2 tbsp arrowroot powder or cornstarch

- 1 cup unsweetened plain organic soy or almond milk

- 2 tsp soy sauce or tamari (for gluten free option)

- salt and pepper to taste

Mashed Potatoes

In a large soup pot add potatoes and enough water to cover them. Boil for about 20 minutes. They are done when you can easily poke them with a fork. Drain the water, and put back into the pot (no heat). Add the thyme (optional), as well as desired amount of salt.

Mash with a potato masher until desired consistency is achieved.

Stores well in a covered glass container in the fridge for 3 - 4 days.

Mushroom Gravy

While the potatoes cook, make the gravy:

In a medium sauce pan over medium heat, add the 1/4 cup of vegetable broth. Once warmed add in the onion, garlic, and carrots. Sauté for 2 minutes adding more vegetable broth if needed to prevent burning.

Add the mushrooms and cook for 5 minutes. Add the fresh thyme and cook 1 more minute.

Add the arrowroot powder or cornstarch and stir until combined with the vegetables cooking for 1 minute and stirring often. Add in the 1/2 cup of vegetable broth, the soy or almond milk, soy sauce, and then mix all until combined.

Bring the mixture to a boil, then reduce to a low heat, about 7 - 10 minutes stirring often. You will know it's ready when the color of the gravy goes from a pale brown to a deeper golden brown.

Remove the gravy from heat once your desired texture has been attained and let sit for at least 5 minutes to allow for more thickening to occur.

Serve potatoes with desired amount of gravy.

Stores well in a covered glass container in the fridge for 3 - 4 days.

Did you know you can boost immunity with mushrooms?

In as little as 1 cup of cooked mushrooms a day, there is a unique array of myconutrients that boost immune function. So try to make mushrooms a steady part of your diet.

PEANUT SOBA NOODLES

Serves 2

Cook noodles according to package directions. While they are cooking, prepare the vegetables and sauce.

In a medium mixing bowl add sauce ingredients and whisk until combined.

Add cooked noodles and toss to combine. Add in vegetables and toss to combine. Add more water to thin if needed.

Garnish with fresh lime, red chili flakes, jalapeño and sesame seeds as desired. These noodles can be served room temperature or cold.

Enjoy!

- 8 oz. soba noodles

- 3 green onions (chopped)

- 1/2 yellow, red, or orange bell pepper (sliced)

- 1 cup carrots (shredded)

- 1 cup zucchini or cucumber (shredded)

Sauce

- 2 cloves garlic (minced)

- 2 tbsp peanut butter

- 1 tbsp tahini

- 2 tbsp rice vinegar

- 1 tbsp soy sauce or tamari (for gluten free option)

- 1/2 tsp maple syrup

- water to thin as needed (1 - 3 tbsp)

Garnish

- fresh lime wedges

- red chili flakes

- jalapeño slices

- sesame seeds

ALFREDO PIZZA
Serves 4

Dough

- 3/4 cup lukewarm water

- 1 tsp active dry yeast

- 2 cups whole wheat flour or whole wheat pastry flour or spelt flour + more for kneading

- 3/4 tsp salt

Alfredo Sauce

- 1/2 cup of raw cashews (soaked and drained)

- 1 tbsp arrowroot starch or tapioca flour

- 2 tbsp nutritional yeast

- 2 cloves garlic

- 1/4 tsp salt

- 1 cup unsweetened plant milk (I used cashew)

Toppings

- portabella mushroom (sliced)

- tomato (sliced)

- spinach (cut into ribbons)

- 2 - 4 garlic cloves (sliced length wise)

- crushed red chili flakes (optional)

- more nutritional yeast (optional)

- vegan shredded cheese (optional as this is a processed food)

Preheat the oven to 450°F and line a baking sheet or pizza pan with parchment paper.

To make the dough, pour the water into a medium mixing bowl and sprinkle the yeast over the water. Let stand for 5 minutes until dissolved and foamy.

Add the flour and salt. Mix with a wooden spoon and then knead with hands until a shaggy dough forms. Turn the dough onto a floured work surface and knead until it forms a smooth tacky ball, about 5 - 8 minutes.

Cover the dough with the upside down bowl, and let it rest while you make the Alfredo sauce and chop the toppings (about 15 minutes).

To make the Alfredo sauce, place all Alfredo ingredients into a high speed blender and blend on high for 1 - 2 minutes until smooth and creamy. Taste and adjust flavors if need be. Set aside.

Chop vegetables for toppings. Roll out the dough with a rolling pin on a floured surface into your desired crust size, thickness, and shape. Transfer to baking sheet.

Transfer sauce to a pan and cook over medium low heat until slightly thickened. This should only take 1 - 2 minutes. Make sure to stir frequently.

Assemble the pizza by putting the sauce, then the vegetables, desired toppings and spices.

Bake in the oven at 450°F for 15 - 20 minutes. Checking the bottom of the crust for your desired crispiness.

Once ready, let cool for just a few minutes then cut into slices and enjoy!

CREAMY TOMATO BASIL PENNE

Serves 6

Preheat oven to 400°F and line a baking sheet with parchment paper.

Place tomatoes, onions, garlic, and a pinch of salt, and pepper onto baking sheet. Stir to combine a bit. Roast for 20 - 25 minutes.

While vegetables are roasting, cook pasta according to package directions. Strain pasta and set aside.

Next, transfer all ingredients on the baking sheet (including juices) into a high speed blender along with soaked and drained cashews and nutritional yeast. Blend until smooth. Taste and add salt and pepper as desired.

Toss pasta with sauce and top with fresh basil, salt, freshly cracked pepper and chili flakes if desired.

- 2 14.5 oz. cans diced tomatoes (drained)

- 1 medium yellow onion (chopped)

- 6 cloves garlic (peeled and crushed)

- 17.6 oz. whole grain penne pasta (brown rice, quinoa, or whole wheat are good options)

- 3/4 cups cashews (soaked and drained)

- 1 tbsp nutritional yeast

- fresh basil (chopped, desired amount to taste)

- salt and freshly ground pepper to taste

- chili flakes to taste

HEARTY LENTIL LOAF
Serves 4

- 1 and 1/2 cups cooked brown lentils (divided into 1 and 1/4 cups, and another 1/4 cup)

- 2 medium onions (chopped)

- 2 large cloves of garlic (minced)

- 1 large carrot (finely chopped)

- 2 tbsp ground flaxseed

- 3/4 cup walnuts

- 1 cup rolled oats

- 2 tbsp tomato paste

- 1/3 cup + 1 tbsp unsweetened soy milk

- 2 tsp soy sauce or tamari (for gluten free option)

- 2 tsp oregano (chopped fresh if possible, but dried will work too)

- 2 tsp thyme (chopped fresh if possible, but dried will work too)

- 2 tsp rosemary (chopped fresh if possible, but dried will work too)

- 2 tbsp (chopped fresh parsley)

- salt and freshly ground pepper to taste

Gravy

- 1 onion (chopped)

- 1 carrot (chopped)

- 2 celery ribs (chopped)

- 1 clove of garlic (minced)

- 2 tbsp tomato paste

- 1 tbsp arrowroot powder

- 1/3 cup dry red wine

- 1 and 1/4 cups vegetable broth

- 1/2 tsp oregano (chopped fresh if possible, but dried will work too)

- 1 tsp ground paprika

- 1/2 tsp rosemary (chopped fresh if possible, but dried will work too)

- salt and freshly ground pepper to taste

Preheat the oven to 350°F.

Cook the lentils according to package direction. Typically 3/4 cup dry will yield about 1 and a 1/2 cups cooked. Divide the lentils into 1 and 1/4 cups and another 1/4 cup for later.

In a large frying pan, add a little bit of vegetable broth or water to sauté the onion and garlic for 2 minutes. Then add the chopped carrots and cook for another 3 minutes.

Put the 1 and 1/4 cups cooked lentils, onions, garlic, carrots, flaxseed, walnuts, oats, tomato paste, soy milk, and soy sauce into a food processor and process until you have a sticky, but still textured mixture. You may have to stop a few times to scrape the sides down.

In a large mixing bowl add the contents of the food processor, the remaining 1/4 cup cooked lentils and season with oregano, thyme, rosemary, parsley, and salt and pepper to taste. Mix together until well combined.

Place the mixture into a loaf pan lined with parchment paper. Bake for 60 minutes.

While the lentil loaf is cooking make the gravy. In a medium sauce pan, add a little bit of vegetable broth or water to sauté the onion and garlic for 2 minutes. Then add the carrots and the celery and cook for another 3 minutes. Stir in the tomato paste and cook until it becomes slightly brown. Then stir in the flour and deglaze with the red wine. Add in the vegetable broth. Season with oregano, paprika, rosemary, salt, and pepper.

Reduce the heat and simmer on low for 25 minutes stirring occasionally. Pour the mixture into a high speed blender and blend on high until smooth. Return to the pot and add more salt or pepper as desired.

Serve on top of the lentil loaf or on the side as a dipping sauce. Enjoy!

Note: *You can make the lentil loaf the night before and reheat it the next day (at 350°F for about 20 minutes). This will ensure a firmer loaf.*

HOW TO MAKE
NO OIL FRIES

Preheat oven to 450°F

Cut potatoes into desired "fries".

Sprinkle with water and toss potatoes with desired seasoning (try garlic powder, nutritional yeast, rosemary, thyme, smoked paprika, cayenne, or cumin).

Spread potatoes in a single layer on a parchment paper lined baking sheet near the top of the oven until browned and cooked through, about 25 minutes.

If using an air fryer, place seasoned fries into air fryer basket at 400°F for about 25 minutes. Use rotisserie option if available.

SWEET POTATO MISO SUSHI

Serves 4

- 2 cups uncooked short grain brown rice

- 1/4 cup rice vinegar

- 1 tbsp raw granulated sugar

- 1/2 tsp salt

- 7 - 9 nori sheets

- 1 - 2 green onions (thinly sliced length wise)

- 1/2 cup red cabbage (chopped)

- bamboo sushi mat is helpful, but not essential

- for dipping you can use low sodium soy sauce, tamari, wasabi etc.

Sweet Potato Miso Filling

- 1 and 1/4 lb. sweet potato (about 4 medium sweet potatoes)

- 3 tbsp chickpea miso

- 1/3 cup unsweetened plant milk

- salt and pepper to taste

Preheat the oven to 400°F. Prick the potatoes a few times with a fork, then place them on a baking sheet. Roast for about 40 minutes or until fork tender.

Cook rice according to package directions. Allow the rice to cool to a warm room temperature. Once the rice has cooled to a warm temperature, add the rice vinegar, sugar, and salt to the rice pot and stir until well combined.

Allow potatoes to cool so you can handle them. Cut in half and scoop out the flesh into a medium mixing bowl. Add the chickpea miso, plant milk, salt and pepper. Use a potato masher or fork to mash to a "smashed" not "silky" consistency. Set aside.

Lay down one piece of nori sheet shiny side down on a clean dry cutting board. Scoop some rice onto the nori sheet leaving about 1/2 inch space on the end closest to you. Then scoop a bit of the sweet potato miso filling on top. Layer some green onion and red cabbage on top of the rice and sweet potato mash, almost in a pyramid shape.

Wet both ends with a little bit of water so they stick together when rolled. Start rolling from the side closest to you (with all the fillings). Use your hands to help you roll tightly until you reach the end. Press the ends firmly together to "glue" the roll together. If it's not sticking, add a bit more water to the edge of the nori sheet.

Repeat "rolling" steps with all rolls until finished and set aside the rolls for about 5 minutes before cutting into desired pieces. Make sure you are using your sharpest knife to cut these, or all the hard work you just did, will be ruined. Serve and enjoy.

Leftovers store well in a glass container with lid in the fridge for the next day.

CREAMY SUN-DRIED TOMATO MUSHROOM PASTA

Serves 4

- 1 medium onion (diced)

- 5 large garlic cloves (minced)

- 1/4 - 1/2 jalapeño (diced)

- 1 cup vegetable broth (I used Rapunzel Bouillon cubes)

- 13.5 oz. can coconut milk (reduced fat or full fat work well)

- 4 cups crimini or baby bella mushrooms (sliced)

- 15 oz. whole grain or brown rice penne pasta

- 1/4 cup sun dried tomatoes (chopped, no oil)

- 1/2 tsp ground paprika

- 2 large handfuls fresh spinach

Garnish

- fresh basil (cut into ribbons for garnish)

- squeeze of lemon juice (optional, for garnish)

- freshly cracked pepper, red chili flakes, and salt to taste

Cook pasta according to package directions. While the pasta is cooking, make the sauce.

In a large soup pot on high heat, use a bit of vegetable broth to sauté the onions, garlic, and jalapeño for 3 minutes, stirring often adding a splash of water as needed to deglaze the pan.

Add remaining ingredients, except for the spinach, bring to a boil then reduce to a simmer with the lid partially covering. Stir occasionally to prevent burning. Stir occasionally for about 10 minutes.

When pasta is al dente, about 12 - 15 minutes, remove from the heat and drain. Add the pasta to the sauce and continue to allow the sauce to cook down to a semi thick consistency, about 10 more minutes. Then add the spinach to the sauce and stir until well combined.

Squeeze on some fresh lemon juice, sprinkle on thinly sliced basil leaves or some red chili flakes if desired, and enjoy!

SWEET POTATO ENCHILADAS

Serves 4

- parchment paper lined baking sheet

- glass or ceramic baking pan (I used a glass 9 x 13)

Red Sauce

- 3 cloves of garlic (chopped)

- 1 cup vegetable broth (1/2 a cup used at a time)

- 1/2 tsp smoked paprika

- 6 oz. can tomato paste

- 1 drop of hot sauce (optional)

- 1 tbsp maple syrup

- up to 1/2 a cup of water (to reach desired sauce consistency)

Toppings / Garnish

- lettuce (chopped)

- tomato (chopped)

- cucumber (chopped)

- 1/4 - 1/2 an avocado (sliced)

- cilantro (chopped)

- green onion (chopped)

- lime wedges

- 2 - 4 tbsp **Queso Dip (p. 116)**

Enchiladas

- 1 large sweet potato (peeled and cubed)

- 1 can of black beans (slightly drained)

- 1/2 tsp ground cumin

- salt and pepper to taste

- 4 - 7 sprouted grain or corn tortillas

Preheat oven to 400°F. Once ready, bake the sweet potatoes on a parchment paper lined baking sheet for 15 - 20 minutes. During this time make the red sauce and doctor up the beans.

In a medium frying pan add a 1/2 cup of vegetable broth and heat on high. Lower heat to medium and add garlic to sauté on medium for 1 - 2 minutes. Add in smoked paprika and the remaining 1/2 cup of vegetable broth, stir. Then add in tomato paste, maple syrup, a drop of hot sauce (optional) and up to 1/2 cup of water to reach a "sauce" consistency (not too runny, not too thick). Once ready, take the potatoes out of the oven and set aside. Readjust oven temperature to 350°F.

Pour the can of beans into a medium saucepan, add 1/2 tsp ground cumin, desired salt and pepper and heat on medium high until bubbling. Turn off the heat. Add the sweet potatoes to the saucepan with the black beans, stir until combined. This will be your enchilada filling.

In the glass baking pan spread enough red sauce to cover the bottom, and reserve the rest for topping the enchiladas.

Assemble the enchiladas by evenly filling each tortilla with the bean / potato mixture then fold each like a little burrito. Place each enchilada seam side down in your baking pan, right next to each other until you have filled up your pan. Use a spoon to evenly distribute the remaining red sauce on top of the enchiladas and fill the cracks too! Bake for 15 - 20 minutes until warmed through.

Make the Queso Dip.

Once cooked, remove from the oven and evenly distribute the Queso Dip on the enchiladas. Garnish with desired toppings and serve. You can even make a little side salad with your garnish veggies if desired.

LOADED BAKED POTATO

Serves 1

- 1 large sweet potato

- desired amount of: **All Purpose Fat Free Cheese Sauce (p. 118)**, and **Staple Salsa (p. 126)**

- steamed veggies of choice

Preheat oven to 425°F. On a baking sheet, prick sweet potato all over with a fork.

Bake until tender, 45 - 50 minutes.

Steam your desired veggies near the end of the sweet potato baking time. Let the sweet potato cool, then split the top open with a knife and top with desired amount of All Purpose Fat Free Cheese Sauce and Staple Salsa. Garnish with steamed veggies.

HOW TO BROWN ONIONS WITHOUT OIL

Heat a nonstick pan over medium high heat for 1 - 2 minutes or until hot enough to sizzle. Making sure the pan is very hot is the key to being able to brown without oil and not having the onions stick to the pan (this also works with green onions, or other veggies like bell peppers).

Add the diced or sliced onions. Use a wooden pancake type spatula to stir. The flat edge helps keep the onions from sticking to the pan.

The bottom of the onions and the pan will begin to brown within 1 minute. Reduce heat to low then continue to stir often and allow the onions to brown for about 4 minutes.

Turn off heat. Add a tablespoon of water and allow onions and water to sit for 1 minute to get all the onions and browning off the pan.

HOMEMADE APPLESAUCE

Serves 1

- 2 gala or honeycrisp apples (cored and diced)

- 4 medjool dates (pitted and chopped coarsely)

- 1/4 tsp fresh lemon juice

- 1/4 tsp ground cinnamon plus more for garnish

- 1 tbsp water

Add all ingredients to a high speed blender and blend on low gradually moving to a medium speed until desired consistency of apple sauce is achieved. I find it helpful to use a tamper if you have one, to really get all of the ingredients blended. You could always do this in a food processor as well.

Serve topped with additional apple pieces and ground cinnamon if desired.

Preheat the oven to 350°F. Place muffin liners into a standard 12 muffin pan. Set aside.

Make the flax egg and set aside for 5 minutes.

In a large mixing bowl, whisk together flour, baking soda, baking powder, cinnamon, salt, and monk fruit sweetener. Then add in the maple syrup, applesauce, flax egg, vanilla, and plant based milk.

Whisk together until just incorporated, making sure no flour patches remain.

Fold in zucchini, until well combined.

Using a large tablespoon, scoop and drop batter evenly into the muffin pan, fill the cups 3/4 of the way full.

Bake for 25 - 30 minutes, depending on your oven. Insert a toothpick to check for doneness - once it comes out clean, they are done.

Allow muffins to cool in the muffin pan for about 30 minutes. Enjoy!

Note: *Because these muffins are oil free, you may find they stick to the muffin liners a bit. But honestly it is a small price to pay for such a healthy oil free muffin.*

ZUCCHINI MUFFINS
Makes 12 muffins

- 2 cups flour of your choice (whole wheat, split, or oat flour)

- 1/2 tsp baking soda

- 1 tsp baking powder

- 1 tsp ground cinnamon

- 1/4 tsp salt

- 1/4 cup monk fruit sweetener

- 1/4 cup pure maple syrup

- 1/4 cup unsweetened applesauce

- flax egg: 4 and 1/2 teaspoons ground flaxseed plus 1/4 cup water whisked together, set for 5 minutes

- 1 tsp pure vanilla extract

- 1 cup plant based milk (I used organic soy milk)

- 1 and 1/4 cups zucchini (peeled and grated)

MOIST BANANA BREAD

Makes 1 loaf

- 4 medium overripe spotty bananas (peeled and mashed) + 1/2 of one more (sliced length wise) for the top of the loaf if desired

- 1/3 cup unsweetened apple sauce

- 1/3 cup monk fruit sweetener

- 1 tsp vanilla extract

- 1 and 3/4 cups whole wheat pastry flour or spelt flour

- 2 tsp baking powder

- 1/2 tsp baking soda

- pinch of salt

- 1/2 tsp ground cinnamon

- 1/8 tsp nutmeg

- 1/4 cup organic soy milk

- 1/3 cup walnuts (coarsely chopped)

- 1/2 cup raisins

Preheat oven to 350°F, and line a loaf pan with parchment paper.

In a medium mixing bowl, mash bananas with a potato masher or fork. Add in the applesauce, monk fruit sweetener, vanilla and mix.

Then add in the flour, baking powder, baking soda, pinch of salt, cinnamon, and nutmeg. Mix well but only until flour is combined, no need to over mix. Add the soy milk and mix again. The batter will be thick and slightly lumpy. If it seems too lumpy, mash the bananas further to your liking.

Add in walnuts and raisin and mix until combined.

Pour into the parchment paper lined loaf pan. If you decide to add the 1/2 banana (sliced length wise), gently place it in the center of the loaf lengthwise and press down very lightly to put it in place. Bake for 50 - 65 minutes (depending on your oven).

When you can stick a toothpick into the center of the loaf and it comes out clean, it is done. Remove from oven and let it cool 10 minutes before slicing.

Store in a cool dry place in a glass container with lid to keep it fresh for 3 - 4 days.

BASIC "NICE" CREAM

Serves 1

Allow the frozen bananas to defrost for 5 - 7 minutes. In a high speed blender, add all ingredients and blend on low gradually moving up to a low medium speed. Continue to add in a bit more milk if needed and use the tamper to reach your desired consistency.

Use a silicone spatula to scoop out and either serve immediately as a soft serve version or pour into a glass container (like a Pyrex loaf pan) and freeze for later.

- 3 ripe bananas (peeled, sliced, then frozen)

- 1/8 - 1/4 cup desired plant milk (I like organic soy, coconut, or almond)

- 1/8 tsp vanilla extract

- 1 tbsp maple syrup

- 2 coconut milk ice cubes

CHOCOLATE
SHAKE

Serves 1

- 1 ripe frozen banana

- 2 coconut milk ice cubes

- 1 and 1/2 cups plant milk

- 1 tbsp cacao powder

- 1 tsp vanilla extract

- 1 tbsp maple syrup

Blend all ingredients in a high speed blender until smooth. To increase thickness, add a few more coconut milk ice cubes as desired.

GOLDEN MILK LATTE

Serves 1

In a small saucepan, add plant milk, ground turmeric, vanilla extract and maple syrup.

Whisk to combine and warm over medium heat. Heat until hot to the touch but not boiling - about 4 minutes - whisking frequently.

Turn off heat and taste to adjust flavor as needed. Serve immediately.

- 1 cup plant milk

- 1 tsp ground turmeric

- 1/2 tsp vanilla extract

- 1 tsp maple syrup

- garnish with cinnamon if desired

QUICK HOT CHOCOLATE

Serves 1

- 1 cup plant milk

- 1 heaping tbsp cacao powder

- maple syrup or monk fruit sweetener to taste

In a small saucepan, add plant milk, cacao, and desired amount of sweetener. Whisk to combine and warm over medium heat.

Heat until hot to the touch but not boiling (about 4 minutes) whisking frequently.

Chai Masala Mix

Place all chai masala mix ingredients into a medium mixing bowl and combine.

Store the chai masala mix in a glass container with lid. It will last for a very long time in a cool dry place.

Chai Tea Latte

Pour all ingredients into a small spouted saucepan. Place over a medium heat. Allow to heat until small bubbles appear around the perimeter of the milk. Stir the chai scraping the bottom to avoid scalding the milk. When milk comes to a small boil turn off heat.

Add sweetener of your choice. Maple syrup or monk fruit sweetener works well.

If you used the black tea, strain, then enjoy this delicious homemade chai tea latte.

Chai Masala Mix - Yields about 3 cups

- 3/4 cup finely ground black pepper
- 1 and 1/4 cups ground ginger
- 1/4 cup ground cinnamon
- 4 tbsp ground cardamom
- 2 tsp ground cloves
- 1 tbsp ground nutmeg
- 1/4 cup ground turmeric

Chai Tea Latte - Serves 1

- 1 cup plant milk of choice
- 1 tsp loose leaf black tea (optional)
- 1/4 tsp chai masala mix

ACKNOWLEDGMENTS

I am very fortunate to have a partner that is supportive in both life and business. We learn together, from one another, and from our experiences. I am incredibly grateful to my husband **Kris** for all of his hard work on this project. He has taken the delicious recipes I created and photographed them so beautifully, they literally make your mouth water as you flip through the pages. His technical expertise and precision to detail have made the design of this book something we are both truly proud of. Kris, thank you for believing in me and bringing this book into being.

A big Thank You to **Caynel** for sponsoring me with the cooking equipment to create these wonderful recipes. For more about Caynel, check out their website: *caynel.com*

And last but certainly not least, I want to thank **YOU** for purchasing this book! My greatest hope is that it will truly help catapult you on your way to weight loss and a healthy life. When you have your health, you have everything. I am so thankful to **God** for allowing me to be a part of, and witness countless people on their journey as they take hold of their health and run with it. If you have enjoyed what I share in this book and it has helped you in any capacity, I would love to hear from you.

For additional resources and free recipes:

- veganmichele.com
- youtube.com/veganmichele
- instagram.com/vegan_michele
- facebook.com/veganmichele

For products and kitchen tools I used in this book, please check out my Amazon Store Front. You can also find my favorite Vegan Beauty and Self Care items, and books to keep you motivated on your journey to health:

- amazon.com/shop/veganmichele

"It does not matter how slowly you go, as long you don't stop." - Confucius